Career Education and English, K–12

NCTE Project on Career Education

Jan E. Kilby, Project Director
Charles Suhor, National Council of Teachers of English,
Administrative Director

Task Force on Career Education

Lori Clarke, University of Utah
Patricia Jo Clayton, Novelist, New Orleans, Louisiana
Marjorie N. Farmer, School District of Philadelphia
Edmund J. Farrell, University of Texas at Austin
Kris D. Gutierrez, University of Colorado
Marjorie M. Kaiser, University of Louisville
Glenn Leggett, President Emeritus, Grinnell College, and Vice
President, Deere and Company, Moline, Illinois (retired)
Jesse Perry, San Diego City Schools
Donna Townsend, Texas Education Agency
Francis W. Weeks, University of Illinois at Urbana-Champaign

Consultant-Readers

Richard Blough, Emmerich Manual High School, Indianapolis
Sheri James Brake, Eureka Elementary School, Missouri
Shirley Haley-James, Georgia State University
Robert Spencer Johnson, Shelter Rock Junior High School, Albertson,
New York
Judy Bloom Uriostegui, San Diego City Schools

Career Education and English, K-12

Ideas for Teaching

Editor

Jan E. Kilby
University of Illinois at Urbana-Champaign
Director, 1978–1979 NCTE Project on Career
  Education

Consulting Editor

Charles Suhor
Deputy Executive Director for Professional
  Programs
National Council of Teachers of English

Project on Career Education
National Council of Teachers of English
1111 Kenyon Road, Urbana, Illinois 61801

Grateful acknowledgement is made for permission to reprint the following material. Figures from *Career Education: A Handbook of Funding Resources,* by Charles W. Ryan. Copyright © 1979 by Houghton Mifflin Company. Reprinted by permission of Time Share Corporation. Excerpt from *Career Education: What It Is and How To Do It,* by Kenneth B. Hoyt, Edward F. Mackin, Rupert N. Evans, Garth L. Mangum. Copyright © 1974 by Olympus Publishing Co., Salt Lake City. Reprinted by permission of Olympus Publishing Co.

The material in this publication was prepared pursuant to a contract from the U.S. Office of Education, U.S. Department of Health, Education, and Welfare. Points of view or opinions expressed do not necessarily represent policies or positions of the Office of Education.

Book Design: Tom Kovacs, interior; V. Martin, cover

NCTE Stock Number 04371
Published in 1980 and distributed exclusively by the National Council of Teachers of English, 1111 Kenyon Road, Urbana, Illinois 61801. Printed in the United States of America.

Library of Congress Cataloging in Publication Data

Main entry under title:

Career education and English, K-12.

   Bibliography: p.
   1. Career education—United States.
2. Career education—United States—Bibliography.
3. English language—Study and teaching—United
States.   I. Kilby, Jan E., 1949-   II. Suhor,
Charles.   III. National Council of Teachers of
English. Project on Career Education.
LC1037.5.C38   375'.0086   80-13157
ISBN 0-8141-0437-1

5 /22 /81 Becheer + Tylr   C. Co

Contents

Preface

English professionals have many opportunities to integrate career education into the K-12 English language arts curriculum to help students understand how the study of English contributes to their total career preparation and to acquaint them with the many careers related directly to the study of English. Teachers, supervisors, and administrators of English programs can integrate career education by infusing the concept into the existing school curriculum and program and by collaborating with other educators, parents, and community members to design experiences to facilitate students' career development. This book contains teaching ideas and curriculum resources to assist English educators to become more actively involved in career education efforts.

Most of the ideas and resources presented were suggested by classroom teachers, supervisors, and administrators of English programs, and by others who have been actively involved in career education. These ideas range from providing students with opportunities to practice writing and reading skills that will be useful in every kind of work, to helping them become acquainted with the theme of vocation in literature, to increasing their awareness of themselves and their career goals, to acquainting them with career opportunities in specific fields.

As editor, I have attempted to select exemplary materials and ideas that are representative of the best, most positive, career education practices for English professionals. The book begins with an introduction that provides general information about career education, the unique role of the English teacher in career education, and the background of this publication. Part I provides exemplary teaching ideas for the three major stages of career development: career awareness (grades K-6); career exploration (grades 7-9); and career preparation (grades 10-12). Each section contains a variety of useful suggestions for integrating career education into the curriculum areas of language, literature, and composition to develop the skills of reading, writing, speaking, and listening. Part II, the resource lists, supplies information about English and career education and about career education in general.

The completion of a book is rarely the accomplishment of only one person; usually many people contribute to its conception, design, and publication. I would like to thank the National Council of Teachers of English for giving me the opportunity to share with English professionals my interest in career education. I have enjoyed my role as director of the NCTE Project on Career Education, and I have especially enjoyed being the editor of this book. All of the staff members of both the Council and the ERIC Clearinghouse at the Council deserve recognition for their many contributions to the project and to this publication particularly. I would especially like to mention Robert Hogan, Executive Director; Jack Maxwell, Deputy Executive Director for National Relations; and Bernard O'Donnell, Director of the ERIC Clearninghouse on Reading and Communication Skills. I also am grateful to the members of the NCTE Task Force on Career Education for their support and guidance in the conception and development of this book, and in all project activities.

Next I would like to express my appreciation of the many people who contributed their ideas and materials for inclusion in this book. These include classroom teachers, supervisors, and administrators in English programs K-12, English educators in colleges and universities, and state supervisors of English language arts and reading, as well as writers and editors of articles, books, curriculum guides, and ERIC documents. Specific mention must be made of those individuals to whom ideas are attributed in Part I: Robert Beck, El Cerrito, California; Gerald Byrd, Henry County Public Schools, Martinsville, Virginia; Clella J. Camp, Kansas High School, Kansas, Illinois; Anita Tapper Eaton, Lt. Job Lane School, Beford, Massachusetts; Jean Hairston, Henry County Public Schools, Martinsville, Virginia; Sandro Ingari, Copiague Public Schools, Copiague, New York; Joyce Kelly, Carbondale Community High School, Carbondale, Illinois; Joseph Sanacore, Hauppauge School District, Long Island, New York; Allen Stessman, Sheboygan Area School District, Sheboygan, Wisconsin; Stephen Thompson, University of Akron, Akron, Ohio; and Jean Ward, New Braunfels Middle School, New Braunfels, Texas.

The state coordinators of career education and educators in other associations and projects also contributed by sharing many excellent materials that were the source of exemplary ideas and suggestions. (These materials—some cited as sources of many of the ideas in Part I—are listed in Chapter 5 under Curriculum Guides.) In addition, I would like to thank the English professionals who served as consultant-readers. Their comments and suggestions were extremely helpful in the completion of the manuscript.

Finally, I would like to thank Charles Suhor, NCTE Deputy Executive Director for Professional Programs, who served as administrative project director, for his many contributions to the development of this book and for sharing with me his understanding of career education and his sensitivity to the needs of teachers.

Jan Kilby

Introduction

One of the several historically important goals of education in our society has been that of education as preparation for work—that significant activity engaged in by the majority of adults in their lifetimes. The goal of education as preparation for work has been consistently evident in the statements of educational purpose of national commissions, associations, and institutions, and in the development of school curricula and programs.

Although the basic belief in the importance of education for career preparation has long been an underlying part of our academic curriculum at all levels, the term *career education* did not evolve until the early 1970s with the emergence of the movement begun by, among others, Sidney P. Marland, Jr. and Kenneth B. Hoyt in their work at the U.S. Office of Education. Since then, school personnel and others have been committing themselves more openly to career education. This commitment has been a way for those concerned about education to respond to a growing number of conditions calling for educational reform. Hoyt describes the nature of this response in the early document, *An Introduction to Career Education: A Policy Paper of the U.S. Office of Education.*

> Career education represents a response to a call for educational reform. This call has arisen from a variety of sources, each of which has voiced dissatisfaction with American education as it currently exists. Such sources include students, parents, the business-labor-industry community, out-of-school youth and adults, minorities, the disadvantaged, and the general public. While their specific concerns vary, all seem to agree that American education is in need of major reform at all levels. Career education is properly viewed as *one* of several possible responses that could be given to this call.[1]

Many of the criticisms of education in the early 1970s focused on some serious problems related specifically to the relationship between education and work: high student drop-out rates at all levels; underemployment and unemployment of graduates; the continuing presence of sex-race-age stereotyping in employment and educational opportunities; inadequate provisions for continuing and recurrent education; and failure of students to experience a smooth transition from education to work.[2]

What, then, is career education and how does it propose to solve these problems in education? Career education has recently been defined as

> ... an effort aimed at refocusing American education and the actions of the broader community in ways that will help the individual acquire and utilize the knowledge, skills and attitudes necessary for each to make work a meaningful, productive and satisfying part of his or her way of living.[3]

Career education as a concept is based on several beliefs. Kenneth Hoyt describes these in the early and now well-known book, *Career Education: What It Is and How to Do It:*

1. Preparation for successful working careers should be a key objective of all education.
2. Every teacher in every course should emphasize the contribution that subject matter can make to a successful career.
3. Hands-on, occupationally oriented experiences should be used, where appropriate, as a method of teaching and motivating the learning of more abstract academic content.
4. Preparation for careers should be recognized as involving and interrelating work attitudes, human relations skills, orientation to the nature of the workaday world, exposure to alternative career choices, and the acquisition of actual job skills.
5. Learning cannot be reserved for the classroom. Learning environments for career education should also be identified in the home, in the community, and in employing establishments.
6. Beginning in early childhood and continuing through the regular school years, allowing the flexibility for a youth to leave for experience and return to school for further education ... career education's time horizons extend from "womb to tomb."
7. Career education is a basic and pervasive approach to all education, but it in no way conflicts with other legitimate education objectives such as citizenship, culture, family responsibility, and basic education.
8. Career education is for all individuals—very young children and the adults of the community, the intellectually able and the mentally handicapped, males and females, those who will attend college and those who will not, the economically affluent and the economically disadvantaged, and those from rural and those from urban settings.

9. Career education seeks to help individuals become familiar with the wide variety of work values now present in society. It imposes no single standard form of work values on any individual. . . .

10. Career education is vitally concerned with helping individuals *implement* their own personal work values. To do this demands that in addition to *wanting* to work, individuals must also acquire the skills *necessary* to work, and having done this, must then find work that is both meaningful and satisfying to them. Thus jobs, in a generic sense, are not career education's goal. Rather, work as productive activity that holds personal meaning and satisfaction for the individual is the ultimate goal of career education.

11. The schools cannot shed responsibility for the individual just because he or she has been handed a diploma or has dropped out. While it may not perform the actual placement function, the school has the responsibility to stick with the youth until he has his feet firmly on the next rung of his career ladder, help him get back on the ladder if his foot slips, and be availale to help him onto a new ladder at any point in the future that one proves to be too short or unsteady.[4]

Career education, then, requires a close partnership among those who play a major role in students' career decisions and career development—that is, among persons in the home, the school, and the community. Career education is based primarily on the concept of career development, which is part of the larger process of human development, extending from infancy to maturity. It involves all of the experiences from which we form ideas, attitudes, and values about ourselves and the world of work, and make career choices.

In recent years, career development theories have been created to account for the way in which this process occurs. Career development theorists typically have identified distinct stages or phases.[5] In the earliest stage of career awareness, approximately from kindergarten through grade six, individuals first become aware of themselves and the environment. In the intermediate stage, in grades seven through nine, youngsters explore in greater depth the careers that are available and they begin to look carefully at their career-related interests, goals, and abilities. In the career preparation stage, grades ten through twelve, individuals actually begin to equip themselves for specific careers.

Much has been written about the crucial role that classroom teachers play in career education. In her monograph, *Career Education and the Teaching/Learning Process,* Barbara Preli writes:

The teacher, as the daily manager of the learning environment, holds the key to the implementation of the concept. Teachers are with the students daily, and they are the most influential in establishing a relationship between education and the world of work. As organizers of learning experiences, they need to include parents, counselors, and members of the community as resources in the learning process.[6]

The two primary strategies for integrating career education into the existing curriculum or school program are infusion and collaboration. By infusing career education into the curriculum or program, teachers can ensure that career education will become an integral part of instruction in all academic areas. By collaborating with parents and members of the community, teachers can design career education activities, programs, and materials that provide students with opportunities to become fully aware of the close relationship between education and work.

In acquainting students with the world of work, teachers may wish to introduce the concept of career clusters. This refers to a standard list, often seen in occupational literature, which was devised to group occupations into clusters by reason of their naturally close relationship. The fifteen career clusters are:

agribusiness/natural resources	hospitality and recreation
business and office	manufacturing
communications and media	marine service
consumer/homemaking education	marketing and distribution
construction	personal services
environment	public service
fine arts and humanities	transportation
health	

The list below may be helpful to English teachers in the classroom, to illustrate some of the many occupations related directly to the study of English in the communication and the fine arts and humanities clusters:

advertising executive	book publicist
advertising copywriter	college teacher
book editor	film critic

high school teacher

librarian

literary agent

magazine editor

newspaper reporter

novelist

playwright

public relations executive

publisher

radio script writer

screen writer

speech therapist

technical writer

television reporter

In recent years, English educators at all levels have expressed a growing interest in career education. Discussions of the relationship between the goals of career education and those of English instruction, as well as descriptions of methods and materials for mutual achievement of these goals can be found in numerous journal articles, books, research reports, and curriculum materials. Many English professionals have participated in career education projects, inservice programs, and conference workshop presentations on career education in their school districts or institutions.

Along with other professional organizations for teachers of English—such as the International Reading Association and the Speech Communication Association—the National Council of Teachers of English has responded to its members' interest in career education. Like other associations, it has commissioned reports, appointed committees, and provided forums for discussion in its publications and conferences. In fact, a brief look at the history of NCTE's involvement in career education shows that it has been especially responsive to the ongoing interest in career education.

As long ago as 1961, NCTE established the Committee on Careers in English for a period of three years to prepare a publication on career opportunities in English for high school and college students. As a result, committee members Robert Carruthers and Hardy Finch edited a leaflet, *Careers in the Teaching of English,* and later the committee chair, Elizabeth Berry, wrote a book, *The Careers of English Majors.*[7]

In 1974, NCTE appointed a Study Committee on Career Education—composed of Dorothy Davidson, Mildred Dougherty, Jesse Perry, Seymour Yesner, and Marjorie Farmer—to represent NCTE at a December 1974 Conference on Career Education for members of seven professional associations of teachers in various academic areas. The conference was sponsored by the National Foundation for the Improvement of Education of the National Education Association and was held at the University of Maryland. The discussions of the NCTE representatives and other participants were recorded and later published in a book, *Career Education in the Academic Classroom,* edited by Garth L. Mangum, et al.[8] The essay by the NCTE representatives, "Career Education in the English Classroom," reflects the early commitment of English professionals to the career education concept.[9] The authors discuss the relationship between the goals of English language arts instruction and goals of career education, asserting that English studies have both humanistic and practical purposes, and career education should thus be an important part of the English curriculum:

> The task of reconciling the human uses of English with the practical applications of English is basic in the profession. The humane uses are to help students define and enhance the self and achieve healthy interaction with others. The practical uses are the means by which the self is presented and by which dynamic interaction with others is achieved. These are the specific skills needed for functional, practical literacy—job applications, employment resumes, interviews, public speaking, and other forms of informational and persuasive communication. A career education emphasis in English can help clarify the interdependence that unites these humane and practical functions.[10]

The authors reached the following conclusions:

> In summary, even as the teaching of English undergoes redefinition, its inherent purpose is steadfast: to give students the opportunity to achieve communication competencies to serve them as adults in seeking personal fulfillment and service to the common good, and in participating creatively and effectively in the life of the community.
> Career education, broadly defined, can penetrate the content and the methodology of the high school English program at a time when students are seeing the need to make career decisions. The English classroom can become a laboratory in which to explore communication in its many forms and to prepare for effective and satisfying communication with other people. These are vital skills, whether they are used in work, in leisure, or in both.[11]

In the fall of 1976, the U.S. Office of Education invited NCTE to send representatives to a Mini-Conference on Career Education for Postsecondary and Association Practitioners. NCTE appointed a Committee on Career Education—composed of Robert Hogan, Dorothy Davidson, Charles Suhor, Francis Weeks, and Marjorie Farmer—to reexamine the interest of English professionals in career education and to attend the February 1977 conference in Bethesda, Maryland.

In the late 1970s, NCTE member interest in career education continued. At the Annual NCTE Convention in New York City in 1977, Dorothy Davidson chaired a three-day preconvention study group entitled "English Language Arts and Career Education."

In 1978, NCTE was invited to apply for a U.S. Office of Education contract to conduct a special fourteen-month project on career education. NCTE was awarded the contract and began the project on October 1, 1978. Its purpose was to involve NCTE members in career education, in response to their expressed interest in such activity. A project office and a national clearinghouse of information on English and career education were established at Council headquarters, and a task force of ten English professionals was appointed to advise the project.

Activities conducted under the project included a one-day preconvention workshop on "Career Education in the English Program, K–12" at the Sixty-ninth Annual NCTE Convention in San Francisco, and the production of four project newsletters entitled *Update on English and Career Education.* A national survey of members' interests, attitudes, and needs relating to career education was conducted in May 1979. In addition, the project included the publication of this book, and another, *Essays on Career Education and English, K–12,* edited by Marjorie Kaiser.[12]

The book in hand is intended as a practical guide for teachers of English, from kindergarten through the twelfth grade, who wish to incorporate career education in their classroom activities. The teaching suggestions came from several sources. Some were submitted by teachers in response to an advertisement in the first project newsletter. Others were gleaned from a computer search of the ERIC collection of documents on the subject of career education in English, K–12. Still others came from a general review of the literature in a search for workable and innovative suggestions. Thus the ideas presented here—usually in adapted form—have been used successfully by teachers in the field in a variety of classroom environments. Most of the activities will be usable in whole or in part by teachers everywhere, or they can serve to stimulate other ideas for teachers who wish to invent activities of their own.

Notes

1. Kenneth B. Hoyt, *An Introduction to Career Education: A Policy Paper of the U.S. Office of Education* (Washington, D.C.: Government Printing Office, 1974; Arlington, Va.: ERIC Document Reproduction Service, ED 097 588), p. 1.

2. Kenneth B. Hoyt, *An Introduction to Career Education,* pp. 1-2.

3. Kenneth B. Hoyt, *A Primer for Career Education* (Washington, D.C.: Government Printing Office, 1979; Arlington, Va.: ERIC Document Reproduction Service, ED 145 252), p. 5.

4. Kenneth B. Hoyt, Rupert N. Evans, Edward F. Mackin, and Garth L. Mangum, *Career Education: What It Is and How to Do It,* 2nd ed. (Salt Lake City: Olympus, 1974), pp. 22-24.

5. Norman C. Gysbers and Earl J. Moore, "Beyond Career Development—Life Career Development," *Personnel and Guidance Journal* 53 (May 1975): 647-652; Samuel H. Osipow, *Theories of Career Development* 2nd ed. (Englewood Cliffs, N.J.: Prentice-Hall, 1973); Donald E. Super, R. Starishevsky, N. Matlin, and J. P. Jordaan, *Career Development: Self Concept Theory* (New York: CEEB, Research Monograph No. 4, 1963); John L. Holland, *The Psychology of Vocational Choice* (Waltham, Mass.: Blaisdell, 1966) and John L. Holland, *Making Vocational Choices: A Theory of Careers* (Englewood Cliffs, N.J.: Prentice-Hall, 1973); Eli Ginzburg, S. W. Ginsburg, S. Axelrad, and J. L. Herma, *Occupational Choice: An Approach to a General Theory* (New York: Columbia University Press, 1951).

6. Barbara Stock Preli, *Career Education and the Teaching/Learning Process* (Washington, D.C.: Government Printing Office, 1977; Arlington, Va.: ERIC Document Reproduction Service, ED 159 355), p. 4.

7. Robert Carruthers and Hardy Finch, eds., *Careers in the Teaching of English* (Urbana, Ill.: National Council of Teachers of English, n.d.); Elizabeth Berry, *The Careers of English Majors* (Urbana, Ill.: National Council of Teachers of English, 1966, out of print; Arlington, Va.: ERIC Document Reproduction Service, ED 159 355).

8. Garth L. Mangum, James W. Becker, Garn Coombs, and Patricia Marshall, eds., *Career Education in the Academic Classroom* (Salt Lake City: Olympus, 1975; Arlington, Va.: ERIC Document Reproduction Service, ED 115 825).

9. Dorothy Davidson, Mildred Dougherty, Jesse Perry, Seymour Yesner, and Marjorie Farmer, "Career Education in the English Classroom," in *Career Education in the Academic Classroom,* eds., Garth L. Mangum, James W. Becker, Garn Coombs, and Patricia Marshall (Salt Lake City: Olympus, 1975; Arlington, Va.: ERIC Document Reproduction Service, ED 115 825), pp. 57-73.

10. Dorothy Davidson, et al., p. 60.

11. Dorothy Davidson, et al., p. 72.

12. Marjorie M. Kaiser, ed., *Essays on Career Education and English K-12* (Urbana, Ill.: National Council of Teachers of English, 1980).

I Teaching Ideas

1 Career Awareness, Grades K-6

Career development, a process that lasts from infancy to maturity, begins as soon as children begin to observe the lives of their family members and the people closest to them. In their earliest interactions with others, children begin to develop attitudes, values, and ideas about themselves and the world around them, which ultimately will influence their major life choices and decisions, especially those regarding their choice of career.

It is important during this stage for those influencing children to provide numerous opportunities for exposing them to a variety of careers, to foster understanding of the importance of work in the lives of individuals and the community, and to begin teaching them the relationship of education to career preparation.

The following ideas and suggestions for achieving these goals have been developed and tested in the classroom by experienced teachers.

A Case Study Approach

To help students understand the roles and responsibilities of all employees within a given organization, such as a hospital, store, church, or hotel, teachers can use the case-study approach. The class can make a preliminary study of their school and identify all of the workers within the school (faculty, administrators, custodians, cafeteria workers, and so on), as well as those who supply goods and services to the school—laundry, paper goods, and food service suppliers. Students can draw a large chart or diagram to illustrate how all of these workers contribute to the operation of the school. The class can then select a typical store, hospital, church, hotel, or other place of business and conduct the same kind of study. In this way, they can come to understand how various people are employed and how each makes a contribution.

3

Career Awareness Activities

Activities such as those described below can enable students to become familiar with the duties and skills of persons in various careers, differences in working conditions, and factors that affect job satisfaction and success.

Students can visit a local factory to learn about the kinds of jobs, requirements for employment, and salary to be expected. Each student can then write a report of the visit and share it with classmates.

Students can choose an occupation or career to research and then play "What's My Line" with classmates. Panelists can ask questions until they receive a negative answer; then the next panelist takes a turn.

Students can learn about career development by reading a biography or autobiography of a famous physician, lawyer, teacher, scientist, politician, or other professional. They can share their findings in a brief oral report to the class, emphasizing why the person chose that career.

Parents of students can be interviewed on a voluntary basis for information about their careers. Students can create a display of pictures and other items illustrating their parents' jobs for the class bulletin board and list training needed, what the parent likes or dislikes about the job, the starting pay, and employment benefits.

Through simulated job interviews with each other, students can practice for real-life job interviews. Students should take turns being the employer and the interviewee. Interviews can be conducted in front of the class.

Posters advertising various occupations within a career field can be created by students and placed around the classroom. For example, students can illustrate specialties in medicine or agriculture.

After students begin to learn about new careers they can examine interesting words and expressions that are part of the jargon of each career field. Lists can be displayed on the bulletin board and pictures relating to the career can be used.

Students can develop a scrapbook about career fields and include pictures, articles, pamphlets, and other materials.

They can write actual business letters to associations or companies to receive career information.

To help students become aware of the particular kinds of dress worn by members of various fields of work, have them come to class wearing typical garments and bringing some job-related accessories. Or, they might wear the uniform of the career field they plan to enter.

Students can develop a mock television script about careers and present the program in front of the class. Students can do research on where to find information about various careers and then create a bulletin-board display of their findings.

After students learn about particular careers, they can write news stories, editorials, special columns, or advertisements about specific careers for their school newspaper. (Source: Sandra Ingari)

Career Clusters

Students in many schools are now learning about the fifteen career families or clusters being used to group many related occupations together. The fifteen clusters are as follows:

agribusiness/natural resources

business

communication

consumer/homemaking education

construction

environment

fine arts and humanities

health

hospitality and recreation

manufacturing

marine service

marketing and distribution

personal services

public service

transportation

These clusters, drawn or pictured on the classroom bulletin boards, can help students see the ways in which many jobs are related. Language arts teachers can invite students to brainstorm about various jobs in each cluster to help them understand the nature of those jobs, and then show them how their language arts skills of reading, writing, speaking, and listening are needed in all clusters.

Using Community Resources

Select a *Speaker of the Week* series and tie in curriculum areas with careers. Ask the students to decide which speakers they would like to hear in one special period each week. Students will develop a sense of responsibility, good listening and recording skills, interview techniques, and the ability to discover relationships between school and the so-called real world. For example:

> Mathematics—"Who uses math skills on the job?" (Plumbers, carpenters, cashiers, insurance salesmen, interior decorators, landscape architects, and so on.)
>
> English and language arts—"Who uses reading, writing, and good speaking skills as a part of their job?" (Politicians, librarians, television and radio announcers, travel agents, authors, lawyers, and so on.)
>
> Science—"What kinds of careers use science skills?" (Electricians, dental technicians, chemists, nurses, laboratory researchers and assistants, and so on.)

Plan a *Job of the Month* series. Pick a different cluster or job family (for instance, communication, recreation, transportation) each month and have students prepare a bulletin board to illustrate all the jobs they can find in magazines, newspapers, books, career education media, or similar materials. Have a few student-selected speakers in, to further enlighten the class. Relate curriculum areas and skills to the various jobs in the discussion that follows. (Source: Sharon Kucinski, ed., *Activity Idea Bank*.)

Ideas for Student Participation

Begin a permanent *career bulletin board* of all careers discussed in the class throughout the year. Include field trip observations, speakers, parents' jobs, jobs mentioned in texts, jobs related to subject areas, and so on. The display could include pictures of people at work, their tools, and a description of the job or the related subject area. Make it a student project to see how many different items can be found.

Start a *class guest book*. Provide a suitable notebook and have students devote a page or two to each speaker during the year, including, if possible, the speaker's photograph and signature, and a brief summary of the information presented for each occupation.

Begin a *class year-book* project in the first weeks of the year and include narratives, photographs, and other information about class trips and speakers, and timely items about each student, school events, class prizes, and other activities related to careers.

Conduct a *"What's My Line"* program. Students can research a variety of careers in small groups and each group can role-play these careers to a panel consisting of members of another small group, using a "What's My Line" game format. This activity stimulates interest in careers, builds library skills, and is an alternative method for integrating knowledge of careers with curriculum skills. (Source: Sharon Kucinski)

Fine Arts and Humanities Career Cluster

Teachers can help students to become acquainted with the many enjoyable and interesting occupations within the fine arts and humanities career cluster. Students can define the words "fine arts" and "humanities," learn about what they contribute to our culture, and then explore the various jobs in the cluster.

A bulletin board, a student scrapbook, or a display on a table can be created to illustrate jobs such as pottery, painting, dancing, theater work, interior designing, sculpting, museum work, and architecture.

Teachers can invite other teachers in the school to visit the class and talk about career opportunities in art, music, physical education, dance, drama, and speech. Or, community performers and artists might be invited to talk about personal experiences related to their careers. (Source: Dorothy Clark, Deborah Crawford, Jeanne LaGrossa, Estelle Matthis, Jennalea Miller, Betty Muench, Velma Warner, and Rosemary Burk, *Just Around the Corner: Career Awareness, A Guide for Elementary Teachers, 3-7.)*

Learning from Biographies

To help students understand how various well-known people came to select their careers and why they remained in their careers, have each student read an autobiography or biography of a person whom he or she admires or one whose career the student is personally considering. Have the student write or give orally a brief report that answers the following questions:

Why did the person choose his or her career?

What special training or education was undertaken?

Who influenced the individual in the choice of a career?

Was hard work or sacrifice necessary to achieve success?

What important personal goals were achieved?

After answering these questions, the student can discuss whether he or she is still personally interested in this career field and why. (Source: Dorothy Clark et al.)

Careers in Book Publishing

Children in elementary schools can learn all about careers involved in the making of books by asking local authors, illustrators, poets, and book editors to speak to a reading class. The children can then write their own story book, proofread it, select a title, and make a binding. The finished copy of the book can be read by children in other elementary grades. A copy can be sent to a publisher for possible publication. (Source: Anita Tapper Eaton)

Learning about Community Workers

There are many materials that can be used to show students the importance of community workers in various occupations. The activities described below can easily be conducted in the classroom with a minimum of facilities. (Source: Sharon Kucinski)

Using toy telephones, students can role-play telephone calls to persons who assist the public in emergencies: hospital clerks, the telephone operator, family, neighbors, and firefighters.

Through role-playing and discussion, students can learn how they themselves can be community helpers at home, on the playground, and in the school.

Students can create a collage of pictures to show how many different community workers come to their homes each week. With cut-out pictures or student drawings of people engaged in the various jobs, they can attach pieces of yarn to connect the house with the workers. Examples might be telephone repairpersons, delivery persons, furniture movers, meter readers, or mail carriers.

Students can choose a "Helper of the Week" and invite a speaker from the community to the classroom or create a bulletin board display to illustrate the person's work.

To help students understand the value of work done by many different people, start a discussion with these two questions: What would life be like without [list a specific kind of worker]? What would we have to do if we didn't have those workers in our community?

Discuss how workers in various occupations are affected by the weather (rain, sleet, snow, drought, hail, sun). Teachers might ask students to consider the work of farmers, fire-fighters, recreation workers in parks and resorts, and so on.

Seeing the Community at Work

Students can learn about the vast array of career opportunities in their local communities by engaging in these projects, which involve active participation.

The class can draw a mural depicting members of the community at work. They should include specific busi-nesses, industries, and familiar persons, and try to identify them in their proper locations in the city. It might be wise to limit the depictions to a particular neighborhood or section of the city.

A small-scale model of the community can be built, to show some of the community members in their work settings. Cardboard, construction paper, crayons, paints, and a large piece of plywood can be useful in this activity.

When they have completed one or both of these activities, the students can write short stories that involve people who supply the important goods and services found in their community. (Source: Dorothy Clark et al.)

Learning to Write News Stories

Students can practice their writing skills and, at the same time, learn how to write stories for newspapers by using the five W's approach. Students can do this assignment:

> Remember the five W's: *What* and *Who* are the most important facts and are always first to be revealed. *Why* usually follows. *Where* and *When* are less important facts, and sometimes may be omitted from a news story.
>
> Write a brief paragraph on your club's meeting to vote for officers, to plan an event, or to conduct some kind of business. Use all the five W's. Proofread your article and submit it to the rest of the class members for reading.
>
> Or, write a news story about something that is happening in your own neighborhood—a garage sale, new neighbors, road and sidewalk repairs, or a problem of concern to your parents or neighbors.

Students' news stories then can be posted on a bulletin board with accompanying drawings or photographs. (Source: *Career Education: The Newspaper, High Intensity Reading Guide, Grade 3*. Florida.)

Literature and Career Education

Literature can be a useful resource for conveying career information to young readers. Teachers should examine the books in the classroom and school library to identify those that deal effectively with the range of career opportunities available to men and women and people of all ethnic minorities.

Many recent research studies have shown that fiction books for children often present a limited portrayal of the realities of the world around them, especially relating to careers and occupations. Far too often, such books present characters, themes, and plots that reveal a sex bias or ethnic stereotype in portraying characters, situations, and action in the world of work. It is important that books with positive attitudes be available to children, especially because career development begins very early and children are influenced by everyone and everything in their environments, at school and at home.

Several associations and publishing houses (Feminist Press

and Scarecrow Press, for example) are devoted to the publication and dissemination of materials that are nonsexist. Teachers can collaborate with librarians in assessing the quality of the school library collection regarding accurate and unbiased presentation of career education concepts and themes.

Our Town at Work

Using the local newspaper or magazines, students can cut out pictures of individual workers in their work settings and display them on a bulletin board. They can attach a blank sheet of paper below each picture where students can write one-sentence job descriptions of the worker. Examples for this activity are travel agents, construction workers, ship navigators, advertising salespersons, painters, doctors, judges, librarians, landscapers, and store managers. (Source: Jeanetta C. Shipp, *Career Awareness, K-6: I Can Be Me from A to Z.*)

Parents as Career Education Resource Persons

Students' parents can be valuable resources for the classroom teacher. At the beginning of the school year or semester, teachers can send home with students a letter asking parents whether they would be willing to serve as resource persons in the classroom. Parents should be asked to identify their careers, to state what topics they could discuss, and when (dates and times) they would be available for class visits.

After all questionnaires are returned, the teacher and students can determine who will be invited to visit the class. When the parent visits the class, the children can be encouraged to ask questions about the career that has just been described. (Source: Douglas A. Hill and Yvonne Johnson, *Career Education in the Elementary Grades.*)

Understanding How Families Work

Children can become acquainted with the idea that all members of a family have to work together to do the chores needed for the family. Some of the following activities might help students to understand this concept. (Source: Sharon Kucinski)

Have students list jobs that have to be done at home and how a family works together to get things done. What jobs could they personally do at home?

In a learning center in the classroom, students can practice jobs they can do at home. They can practice setting a table correctly, answering the telephone, folding clothes from a clothes dryer, and making a bed. Volunteer parents can assist the teacher in this activity.

Students can discuss the concepts of cooperation, economic interdependence, and responsibility in family life.

Vocabulary of the News Room

Children can learn about careers by becoming acquainted with the jargon or trade expressions used by people in various kinds of work. They will discover many interesting things about the newspaper industry, for instance, by learning the meaning of words such as those listed below. (Source: *Career Education: The Newspaper*. Florida.)

> action shot: picture taken of an event while it is happening
>
> assignment: the story a reporter is told to cover
>
> banner head: front-page headline
>
> beat: area covered by a single reporter
>
> bulletin: an important news story that is received just before or soon after the newspaper is ready to be printed; usually put on page one
>
> caption: lines of type, placed under or near a picture, that tell something about the picture
>
> column: short lines of type arranged vertically on the pages of a newspaper to make it easier to read
>
> cut: to shorten a story (verb); a picture (noun)
>
> deadline: a set time when all stories must be finished if they are to go into a particular issue of a newspaper
>
> editorial: a story that expresses the opinion of the writer or the newspaper in which it appears
>
> final copy: a news story that has been corrected by the editor and is ready to be set into type for printing in the newspaper

five W's: the main parts of a news story: what, who, why, where, when, and sometimes how

follow-up: a story to be continued next day (or issue)

kill: do away with a story or part of it

layout: a plan to show where the stories, pictures, advertisements, and other items are to be placed on a newspaper page (also called a dummy)

lead: first paragraph of a story, giving most of the important information; also, the most important news story in the paper, located in the right-hand column at the top of page one

printers: people who print newspapers

proofreading: correcting all mistakes in spelling and punctuation before the newspaper is printed

scoop: a story one newspaper has that others failed to print

sheet: newspaper

AP and UPI: news offices located in various major cities in the United States and overseas, from which newspapers in other locations can get news from all over the world

Who Works at the Newspaper?

To help students become acquainted with the many jobs involved in creating, producing, and distributing the local newspaper, teachers can conduct a lesson or unit around the careers in the newspaper industry. Some of these occupations can be explored:

owner	photographer
publisher	printer
editor	typist
managing editor	delivery person
reporter (sports, news)	artist
copy editor	

Teaching materials can be obtained from the Newspaper in Education Program of the American Newspaper Publishers Association Foundation, The Newspaper Center, Box 17407, Dulles

International Airport, Washington, DC 20041. (Source: *Career Education: The Newspaper*. Florida.)

Why People Work

Students can become acquainted with the many different reasons why people work in particular jobs by interviewing family members or friends. Various reasons can be discussed, including money, fringe benefits, personal satisfaction, convenient work location or working hours, or retirement or pension plans. Students will probably see that there are several factors affecting career choice. (Source: Dorothy Clark, et al.)

Why We Go To School

Teachers can help students understand how education develops the many skills, attitudes, and knowledge areas needed for career preparation, by asking students to consider how they themselves are being prepared by the school. Teachers can draw a large picture of a school on the blackboard or on a piece of paper and ask each student to write on the picture, giving one way in which school helps them prepare for the world of work. (Source: Dorothy Clark et al.)

Workers and Their Jobs

Students can come to understand the importance and value of creative work to themselves by engaging in a classroom activity in which they design and create an original picture, craft, or story. Students can be asked to bring to class materials for an original piece of work and they can demonstrate to the class just how they design and create the work. After all students have given demonstrations, they can describe how they feel after having created something.

Teachers can then relate this discussion to the feelings of all workers who design, create, and produce goods or services for the community—such as feelings of accomplishment, self-worth, and contribution to themselves or to society. Teachers can add comments about the idea of doing work that is not just routine, but brings a person enjoyment and satisfaction. (Source: *Hawaii Career Development Continuum, Curriculum Guide for Grades K-3.*)

Workers' Responsibilities

Early in elementary school, students can begin to become aware of the meaning of work and the many responsibilities of workers in various occupations. Students in grades K-6 should have opportunities to learn that all workers—whether in the home, school, or community—have rights, privileges, and responsibilities.

Teachers can begin by discussing the rights and responsibilities of students in their own school room, in relation to themselves and their classmates. They can be asked to identify ways in which they fulfill their responsibilities, such as taking proper care of their school supplies and desk area, treating their classmates with respect, and using their time wisely.

Students can then discuss their rights and responsibilities— and those of their brothers, sisters, and parents—at home. Finally, they can discuss their civic and social responsibilities in their community—for instance, obeying traffic and road signals, treating people with respect, and considering the health and safety of those around them.

At the end of these discussions, students can write short paragraphs listing the ways in which people exercise their rights and responsibilities in their work. (Source: *Hawaii Career Development Continuum.*)

2 Career Exploration, Grades 7-9

After youngsters acquire a basic awareness of themselves and the world of work, they begin to explore in greater depth the many career opportunities available to them. They are more aware of their individual interests, goals, abilities, and values, and the skills, attitudes, and knowledge required in various professions and trades. During this stage of career development, students begin to think about careers for themselves, and they have a strong interest in reading about specific careers, in talking to people about their jobs, and in imagining themselves doing certain kinds of work.

Communication Skills on the Job

As students develop the communication skills of reading, writing, listening, and speaking in their English language arts classes, they can discover just how important these skills are in work situations. Some of the following activities may be helpful. (Source: *Communication Skills for Career Education. Junior High/Middle Schools*. Washington.)

> In small groups, students can develop a list of personality traits and work habits that make a person fit into a work team (for instance, acceptance of criticism, loyalty, promptness, and attendance). Discuss the importance of interpersonal relations skills.
>
> Groups of students can role-play on-the-job conflict situations as prepared by other groups, and analyze the success or failure of people to communicate effectively.
>
> Students can write a few paragraphs or a short paper analyzing their own ability or inability to communicate effectively with those in school, at home, or in the community. Ask them to determine when and why they seem to

have problems in communicating with people. Then discuss how they can improve their ability to communicate.

Three students can role-play situations in which two of them pretend to have a disagreement in a work situation and the third student intervenes to try to resolve the conflict. For example:

A customer at a sales counter is waiting to be served and encounters a very slow sales clerk and becomes upset. The store manager enters the area and attempts to intervene. Another example: A busboy in a restaurant spills food on a customer. The customer becomes highly irritated and the manager enters the area to intervene.

A Career Ladder: "Where I Want to Be"

Ask students to think about the various career choices they will make during their lifetimes. Using the ladder chart, each student can fill in his or her career ambitions, ranging from step one—the least expectation at the beginning of the student's career—to step ten at the top of the ladder—the final goal the student hopes to achieve. The object of the exercise, as illustrated in the example below, is to develop a realistic appreciation of the many kinds of work that usually are involved in developing a successful and satisfying career. (Source: Helen S. Hindman and Marion L. Triem, *Career Education in Junior High English.*)

Step 10: Own my own company with a variety of design lines.

Step 9: Write a book on fashion and begin working on plans to start my own business.

Step 8: Become a fashion writer or editor for a magazine.

Step 7: Be a women's wear fashion writer for a newspaper and work as a designer of women's clothes on a free-lance basis.

Step 6: Work for a large clothing design firm in New York City.

Step 5: Become a dress designer in my home town.

Step 4: Become a buyer for women's clothes.

Step 3: Manage a women's wear department in a store in in my town.

Step 2:   Work in a department store in women's wear.

Step 1:   Work in a department store.

Careers for Good Speakers

Many students do not realize the importance of good speech skills in various careers. To develop their understanding of the value of effective speech skills, conduct the following activity. (Source: Katie E. Gilliland and Jeanne Jehl, *A Career Education Unit for Junior High School: Careers for Good Speakers: Communications and Media Cluster.*)

> Have students identify ten different occupations requiring some training in public speaking, either in high school or college.
>
> Have students list the educational requirements needed in order to enter these occupations and the speech skills needed for advancement.
>
> Have students discuss the nature of the work and services or goods provided by people in these jobs, and find examples of how speech skills can affect performance.
>
> Have students discuss community need for the services and goods provided.

Exploring Occupational Stereotypes

As junior high or middle school students learn about careers, they are undoubtedly exposed to the many occupational stereotypes. The media—television, radio, film, and print—frequently present negative or distorted portrayals of people in various occupations. Since students at this age are beginning to develop values and fundamental ideas about work and specific occupations, this is a good time for teachers to help students understand the differences between the stereotypes and reality.

Have students discuss or write about occupational stereotypes as observed in any of the various media, and discuss how and why the stereotypes are used. Then ask them to interview people in these occupations or read vocational guidance reference materials, such as the *Dictionary of Occupational Titles* and the *Occupational Outlook Handbook,* to determine whether there is any reality to the stereotype. (Source: *Getting Started: A Guide to Writing Your Own Curriculum*. Pennsylvania.)

Family Job Roots

Since many people have become interested in examining their family's roots, it is also a good timè to explore the family's job roots. Students should begin with the jobs of their sisters, brothers, and parents, and work back to the jobs of their grandparents, aunts, and uncles. A tree diagram can be used to illustrate changes in kinds of jobs held through the three generations. Students will enjoy using oral interviews with relatives or writing to relatives to seek information. Pictures and newspaper and magazine articles also can be used. Students should try to determine whether jobs and career choices of family members are related and, if so, what factors account for this similarity of choice.

Where to Find Career Information

Many school libraries have vertical files containing pamphlets and brochures about particular subjects such as career fields. Students can explore these materials in conjunction with reading library books, and then use this information in writing research reports, conducting oral presentations before the class, and preparing for interviews with community business persons. Teachers, guidance personnel, and librarians can review the files to see what materials are currently available and what items need to be ordered. (Source: Steven Thompson)

Jobs: Here Today, Gone Tomorrow

Each year approximately 10,000 new jobs emerge in response to the rapid changes in society. To help students understand the past and anticipate future job trends, have them create a bulletin board display or notebook illustrating ten jobs that once existed but are now obsolete, ten jobs that exist today but will soon become obsolete, and ten new jobs predicted for the future. Have them list five to ten conditions in society (economic, technological, social, political) that bring about these changes in job demand. (The *Occupational Outlook Handbook,* usually found in the school guidance office or library, is a good resource for this activity.)

As a related activity, ask the students to define and analyze the changes that take place within a job category. Some goods and services in society have had a long tradition, yet the nature of the work done in providing them has changed radically. Have the students create a bulletin board display or write a report on a product or service (such as laundry or drycleaning, medicine and nursing, or automobile production) and illustrate the changes that have occurred in the worker's role, working conditions, salary and benefits, and equipment needed in production. Information can be obtained from encyclopedias and other reference books, history books, and guidance and vocational literature.

Research Methods to Explore Careers

Students in junior high or middle school can gain experience in research techniques while gathering information for oral or written reports on careers. The exercise outlined below encourages individual effort and originality as well as group activity.

Begin the search for information with a class discussion in which the students compile a list of places to visit and people to call, write, or interview in regard to careers. Encourage suggestions from a variety of fields, in labor and in the professions.

Ask the students to organize their sources, to help them decide where to start the information-gathering process. For instance, start with sources close at hand and then go to those that are less familiar: sources within the classroom, the school library or counseling office, and at home; sources in the community (library, colleges, businesses, civic groups); sources outside the community (unions, associations, state and federal governments).

Ask each student to choose a career and explore its possibilities, adapting the ideas brought out in the group sessions to the individual's own plan of action. Encourage the student to make personal visits or interviews, and to write or telephone businesses and agencies for brochures.

Ask the students to organize their findings and report their results to the class by giving a speech or reading a paper.

Communications Jobs for All Media

Following is a list of teaching ideas for acquainting students
with the many occupations within the communication career
cluster. All of the media for mass communication are represented
in the suggestions. (Source: Joan Soper, ed., *A Career Education
Idea Book for English Teachers*.)

Record five minutes of videotape of a classmate delivering
a news broadcast you have written, and play the tape back
through the television set. Tape must meet acceptable stan-
dards of video and audio reproduction.

Demonstrate the ability to send at least a twenty-five-word
message in Morse Code.

Pretend that you are an "information operator" for the
telephone company. Demonstrate your telephone etiquette
and resourcefulness in locating data by filling at least ten
requests "called in" to you by your classmates.

List at least ten means of communication between two or
more people. Give a brief description of each.

List twenty terms related to television—define each of the
twenty.

Prepare the technical writing necessary to instruct someone
how to build a console for a stereo of predetermined design.

Design three potential covers for this year's yearbook.

Compile a notebook containing samples of printed materials
which you have made using at least three different printing
techniques.

Give a short demonstration of the operation of a tape
recorder.

Give a demonstration of the uses and mechanics of the
Instamatic Camera.

Do an on-the-job interview with a television news camera-
man. Go with him on a story. Record all your activities on
tape and slides.

Contract with the audiovisual coordinator to operate the
audiovisual equipment requested by a teacher.

Record five minutes of videotape illustrating the activities of one, or a group of classmates. Demonstrate competency in filming both long-range shots and close-ups.

Design, illustrate, and label the cartoon page for the school newspaper.

Organize, plan, and publish a weekly newsletter.

Prepare and record a two-minute commercial on a product you have designed and produced.

Prepare a three-page guide of the audiovisual equipment available in this school.

Visit a cinema or movie theater with a camera. Talk to the projectionist and ask for a demonstration of how a movie projector operates. Ask what the projectionist's other duties are and report back to class.

Visit a local television station. Talk to the film editor and ask what the job entails. Talk to a projectionist at the television station. Is the job different from that of the film editor? Does a station require a license, and if so, why?

Lay out an advertising page for a sale at a large local department store.

Make a three-minute commercial, advertising a particular radio station (use a tape recorder).

List ten careers in journalism. Give a one-sentence description of each.

Write a business letter to a television station, asking to interview a broadcaster.

You want to become an apprentice in a printing trade. List the jobs available to you and what you would have to do to be accepted into an apprenticeship program.

Send for information from two to five broadcasting schools and prepare a report for the class which includes benefits and weaknesses of this type of training. Include what points you should check before signing up for one of these courses.

Interview a graduate of a broadcasting school, asking about personal reactions to the school, training provided, help in employment, and any discrepancy between promises and results.

Describe the steps you would have to go through to have a record made of a song you have written.

Spend a day with an advertising account executive and write a first-hand impression of the job duties, skills, and responsibilities.

You are a reporter. Write an article for the school paper covering either an athletic event or a club meeting.

Write and tape a thirty-second advertisement for any product you choose.

Write, blockout, cast, rehearse, and tape a sixty-second television commercial for any product you choose.

List the English skills necessary to work in the production department of an advertising agency.

You are a manuscript. Relate in a first person conversational diary the steps you go through to become a finished book.

Write an editorial on a school or local issue.

Find out the five W's of newspaper writing. What makes good news?

You are a telephone operator. A young child is on the phone and seems to be in trouble. Write a report on what you would do.

List four rules of courtesy when speaking on the phone.

You are a linesman for the telephone company. Relate some of your experiences and job training in the form of a short story.

Write a news article covering a school or local event.

Create an editorial cartoon concerning a school or local issue.

Put together a news team and do a news broadcast (national and local) and include weather and sports.

You are a disc jockey for a local radio station. Make up a fifteen-minute session using monologue, records of your choice, and a commercial.

Talk to a telephone repair person. Find out some advantages and disadvantages of the job.

You are preparing a tape for a recorded telephone answering service. Give the necessary information about the organization concerned.

Describe the various telephone systems now available.

Design a poster to be used to advertise a restaurant.

Watch three television programs of your choice and then write a critical review of each.

You have just been hired to write an advertisement for a shopping mall in order to promote customer interest. Compose an ad that will make people want to shop there.

Choose advertisements for at least fifteen different consumer products. Make a display of the ads and identify the basic human need toward which each is directed.

A Mini-Internship Program

Language arts students from middle school through the high school years can combine classroom study of careers with off-campus study in a mini-internship program, to gain a better understanding of the realities of the world of work and the knowledge, attitudes, and skills needed for employment.

A school can establish a cooperative education agreement with local businesses to give a student a short internship (four days or so) in a job of his or her choice. In preparation for their internships, students formulate a list of objectives for studying the particular career, both in and out of the classroom. They first conduct extensive research, using the resources of the school to prepare them for the job in question. They are then placed with supervisors in a work site and learn as much as they can about the career.

After returning to their classes, students share their experiences with other students in either oral or written reports and form some conclusions about the career. This provides an excellent opportunity for first-hand exposure to a career at an early age. When centered in the language arts curriculum, this program gives students opportunities to use all their communication skills. (Source: Allen Stessman)

The Glamour of Careers

Students, like others, tend to glamorize certain careers such as those in the theater, film, music, professional athletics, or modeling. Society often encourages this tendency by idealizing one facet of a career field at the expense of other jobs in the same field that also demand certain levels of talent and training. For example, students may know a great deal about the work of attorneys through reading the newspapers or watching television, but they may know little about the work of court reporters, legal secretaries, law clerks, and judges. Here are three ideas that use reading and communication skills to guide students toward a more realistic appreciation of the significance of all kinds of work within a given career field.

Have students create a bulletin board display to illustrate the less well-known occupations within a career cluster. Ask the class to discuss the jobs and the part each plays in the overall performance of that particular field of work.

To illustrate how so-called stars often change their careers along the way, ask the students to write a biographical sketch, give a dramatic presentation, or create a bulletin board display to show how this happened to a particular individual—for example, an athlete or a figure skater, who went from amateur and professional status as a performer, to being a sports broadcaster or writer, and finally, to serving as athletic director in a school or college, or coach or manager of a professional team. Students can discuss the relationships of one job to the other, and when and why major changes in career occurred.

Ask students to collect articles from current magazines such as *People, Glamour, Time, Downbeat,* and *Newsweek,* that provide an inside look at the realities of the careers that are generally regarded as glamorous. Discuss the hard work, inconvenience, and personal sacrifice endured by some prominent figures in achieving fame.

The Making of a Hamburger

This activity is effective in showing students that many inter-related jobs are involved in the creation, production, and distribution of a single product:

Ask students to write the story of a hamburger, identifying the many workers that are associated with the process of supplying hamburger meat to their school cafeteria. Ask them to describe the workers in the order in which they performed their chores, from the cafeteria to the farm or ranch.

Students will probably identify at least some of the following jobs: cook, delivery-truck driver, loading-dock worker, freezer locker worker, packager, pattymaker, grinder, meat cutter, meat inspector, chilling room worker, carcass cutter, skinner, slaughterer, stock-yards worker, inspector, livestock buyer, stock-truck driver, rancher, ranch hand, farmer, feed store owner, veterinarian, farm machinery operator, repairperson.

To enlarge upon the activity, the teacher may divide the class into groups to develop descriptions of jobs involved in making or producing the hamburger bun, french fries, salt, pepper, lettuce, tomatoes, and onions. (Source: Helen S. Hindman and Marion L. Triem)

Trace Someone's Job History

Teachers can help students to understand that many individuals change their jobs many times during a lifetime. Ask the students to write job histories of two people they know, using interviews to gather information concerning the various jobs held by each person, from the first job up to the most recent. Encourage the students to look for the causes and effects of career choices and changes.

As a variation, ask the students to imagine that they have just retired and someone has asked them about their job histories. Ask them to outline the various jobs they hope they will have held in a lifetime of work, and to identify the possible causes and effects of their career choices and changes. (Source: Helen S. Hindman and Marion L. Triem)

Guest Speakers on Videotape

When community members come to classrooms to talk with students about careers, students learn a great deal about both the person and the career. Such professionals are busy people, however, and cannot be expected to return each time there is a new class. To ensure that future students will also benefit from the visits (and to give the students some experience in the use of an electronic medium), the guests' speeches can be recorded on videotape for later viewing by other classes. The teacher can provide each speaker with an outline before the visit and ask the guest to emphasize the ways in which communication skills are important in his or her career. This can include the use of teletype, dictating machine, telephone, and the various kinds of paperwork—forms, memos, letters, and reports. (Source: Jean Ward)

3 Career Preparation, Grades 10-12

At the high school stage of career development, students have acquired a basic awareness of careers and of themselves, and they are beginning the process of preparing for one or more careers in which they have interest and ability or talent. They begin to set specific goals and analyze the decisions they must make to achieve those goals. They also become aware of the practical aspects of job seeking—interviewing, writing data sheets and resumes, completing job applications—whether for part-time or full-time, temporary or permanent, employment.

During this stage, too, students carefully analyze the courses they are taking in school because they know that their choice of curriculum is an important part of their preparation for the work they hope to do. They begin to see specific courses as providing them with knowledge, attitudes, and skills needed for employment, either upon graduation from high school or following additional training or education.

Analyzing Career Goals

Teachers can encourage some realistic career planning by asking students to describe their career goals and how they plan to reach them. Students should be encouraged to explore whether the jobs they hope to have will exist in the future, using information from current vocational materials, from school and community libraries, and from persons currently holding such jobs in their community. Such career investigation can help students become more realistic in their career choices and more analytical toward the steps involved in preparing for careers. (Source: Robert Beck)

Career Choice and Life-Style

Students can learn that career choice is one of the most important choices people make because it greatly influences the individual's

way of life—or life-style, as it has come to be called. The suggestions below should help them grasp this concept. (Source: *Hawaii
Career Development Continuum.*)

> Have students define the meaning of the word *life-style* and
> ask them to name some of its elements: choice of living
> environment (rural, urban, suburban), style of dress (formal,
> informal, casual), amount of travel, entertainment prefer-
> ence, social relations, family, choice of work, and so on.
>
> Then ask students to write short essays describing the
> life-style they want to follow, and the abilities and career
> choices that will allow them to achieve it. Students can use
> reference materials from the library or counseling office to
> examine career choices. Be sure to ask students to consider
> whether their choice of career will be compatible with the
> other elements of their life-style.
>
> Or, have students read an article, poem, or book in which
> the main character's job or work environment is emphasized,
> and have them examine how the choice of work relates to
> the character's life-style. Ask whether the individual's career
> determines, or is determined by, other elements of the
> life-style.

Career English Courses

Although career education concepts are generally integrated into
the existing curricula of subjects such as English, some schools
provide additional short courses in so-called Career English, in
which career-related concerns are the focal point for the development of language arts skills. In such courses, students have
opportunities to use their communication skills to explore their
career-related interests, goals, and values, to conduct research
about specific careers, and to become more familiar with the
knowledge, attitudes, and skills needed to become employed.

Such courses typically include a research project in which
students explore specific careers and identify education requirements, working conditions, salaries, occupational outlook, and
worker satisfaction. Additional activities can include the examination (using standardized instruments) of students' interests

and preferences as they relate to work, participation by members of the community as guest speakers, interviews with community business persons, and the creation of classroom displays and bulletin boards, illustrating the theme of work and specific careers, both traditional and nontraditional. Students can also study and discuss the theme of vocation as it is depicted in various literary works.

In such courses, students practice their communication skills by writing business letters of inquiry and application for jobs, completing real job applications, applying for social security cards, writing to persons who might serve as job references, preparing data sheets and complete resumes, conducting research on various careers, locating sources of information about careers, and analyzing the types of careers and the values they represent. Teachers can find many useful articles, books, photographs, cartoons, and bulletin board display items from current magazines such as *Time, Newsweek,* and *People,* from newspapers such as *The New York Times* and *The Wall Street Journal* and the local newspaper, and from books such as Studs Terkel's *Working.*

In these courses, students can learn a great deal about themselves and the world of work and the factors involved in the career decision-making process. (Source: Joyce Kelly. Also, Janet Williams, *Curriculum Guide for Career English.*)

Independent Study Courses

Independent study courses in career investigation can provide students with opportunities to explore specific careers of interest to them. Under the supervision of an interdisciplinary team of faculty, administrators, and support staff, students conduct an individualized research project and receive guidance in research and writing techniques. The final project report is reviewed by the team and after the report is accepted, duplicate copies are placed in the library for other students to read. For this experience, many schools grant one-quarter or one-half credit towards graduation. (A more complete description of this course at Hauppaugue High School, Hauppauge, Long Island, New York, can be found in *Phi Delta Kappan,* February 1978, pp. 403–404.) (Source: Joseph Sanacore)

The Newspaper in the Classroom

One of the most interesting examples of educational collaboration between schools and the community is the well-established Newspaper in Education program of the American Newspaper Publishers Association Foundation. Through this program, local newspaper firms supply students with class copies of newspapers for study in English classes. And one of the best uses of the program is its value in helping students learn about the careers involved in the production and distribution of newspapers.

Teachers can contact the Newspaper in Education representative at their local newspaper if they wish to participate in the program. Often this includes special workshops for teachers on the uses of the newspaper. Teachers also receive informative course outlines, bibliographies of books on the topic, and classroom materials to use with the unit. English teachers can also consult the school's journalism instructor for suggestions regarding the use of these methods and materials, and they should also contact the language arts supervisors in their school districts for sample curriculum guides on the use of the newspaper.

Jobs in Newspaper Publishing

The newspaper industry has many jobs to offer today's students, some for those with a high school education and others requiring additional education. Teachers can direct students toward information about jobs to suit a wide range of interests and abilities, whether in the editorial, business, or production aspects of newspaper publishing. The many possibilities for discussion are indicated in the list that follows. (Source: Robert Megow, Bill Ripley, and Patricia Arredondo, *Newspaper Careers. Occupational Information Package.*)

Editorial	Business reporter
Ad layout person	Camera operator
Ad copy writer	Cartoonist
Art editor and critic	Classified ad clerk
Artist	Columnist
Beat reporter	Copy person
Book reviewer	Copycutter
Business/financial editor	Copyreader

Correspondent

Clerk

Executive editor

Fashion editor

Feature writer

Foreign correspondent

Librarian

Managing editor

News editor

Photo editor

Photographer

Proofreader

Reporter

Society editor

Sports editor

Sports photographer

Sports writer

Business

Accountant

Advertising salesperson

Delivery person

Personnel director

Publisher

Purchasing agent

Secretary

Truck driver

Production

Hand compositor

Layout person

Linotype operator

Machinist

Photo engraver

Plate maker

Press operator

Retoucher

Teletype operator

Chaucer and Career Education

Chaucer's *Canterbury Tales* provides students with a wealth of information about life in the Middle Ages. The many occupations of the era illustrated by the portraits of the pilgrims are most interesting. A career education unit plan for use with the *Canterbury Tales* might include some of the following activities. (Source: Jean Hairston and Gerald Byrd)

Students can illustrate the pilgrims' professions or occupations on a bulletin board or table display. They can describe the nature of the work in each instance and relate it to conditions in the Middle Ages.

Ask students to determine which of the occupations presented in the *Tales* actually exist today in some form.

Students can research and illustrate the costumes, accessories, hairstyles, and other features of the pilgrims as they relate to their occupations.

Students can examine the *Tales* for occupational stereotypes that existed during Chaucer's time and can ponder the statement, "Human nature has changed very little since Chaucer's day."

Students can write and illustrate their own Occupational Handbook of Medieval England based on their reading of the *Tales* and their study and research on medieval England. Some of the occupations they may want to consider are: apothecary, charcoal seller, candlewright, copyist, jester, saddler, or scribe.

Creating Newspaper Advertisements

In some communities, local businesses sponsor a yearly contest for high school students in creating newspaper advertisements. Students in English classes can be encouraged to write their own advertisements and test their ability to use their artistic and linguistic skills effectively. Students begin their projects by selecting a particular product or service to advertise, and a particular store or business that supplies the product or service in their community. They then design advertisements to attract the newspaper readers' attention. The school art or business teacher or a panel of persons from the community can act as judges for the entries, and the best advertisement can perhaps be used in the local newspaper. (Source: Susan Glahn and Clyde Welter, *BO-CEC English Resource Guide.*)

Forms, Forms, Forms!!

Part and parcel of everyday living is the need to cope with a mass of paperwork. There seem to be forms to fill out or forms to read for every sort of activity: applying for goods and services, buying a car, opening a bank account, leasing an apartment, obtaining a job or a driver's license. Students can prepare to meet this need by developing their writing and reading skills in dealing with sample forms obtained from local business firms or purchased at an office supply store. The teacher can provide assistance in defining the legal and technical terms and abbreviations used. A local attorney, bank officer, or credit counselor might be invited to speak to the class. (Source: *New Directions in English.* Oklahoma.)

Getting Ready for Future Shock

Both the book and film of Alvin Toffler's *Future Shock* can be used to help students to think about the inevitability of change in society, and to anticipate the changes that are likely to occur in their lifetime. Such changes would certainly affect the entire field of work because of new developments in technology, shifts in social patterns, use of alternative sources of energy and raw materials, and so on. To gain an understanding of such events, students can select one part of life that Toffler deals with—for instance, education, social relations, or political life— and write about projected changes for the 1980s and beyond. Reference materials such as World Futures Society publications, particularly *The Futurist,* and other magazines and books can be used to support their assessments. (Source: *Getting Started: A Guide to Writing Your Own Curriculum.* Pennsylvania.)

Hobbies, Crafts, and Careers

In this era of do-it-yourself, anyone's hobby or trade might earn them extra money if they can think logically and write well. The project outlined below introduces students to the possibilities of a career in free-lance writing, and it motivates students to improve their writing skills by using them to interest others in a favorite craft or hobby. (Source: *Getting Started: A Guide to Writing Your Own Curriculum.* Pennsylvania.)

> Quote going rates of payment for do-it-yourself articles from various magazines, then show some examples. Analyze the articles by asking: Which ones have more appeal? Why? What is the value of pictures and diagrams along with written instructions? What audience does the writer wish to approach? Will readers have the necessary tools and materials? What will the project cost? What level of skills is required?
>
> Ask the students to choose one of their hobbies and use it as the subject of a do-it-yourself article. Choose a publication and an audience, list materials and tools needed, approximate cost, and then write detailed step-by-step instructions for the project. Use pictures and diagrams, not only for appeal but for clarity.

Writer's Market and *Literary Market Place* can be used as reference materials. The teacher also may use this as a time to explain plagiarism. At the end of the exercise, ask the shop teacher or other appropriate persons to assist in evaluation of the students' projects.

A Career Information Package

A language arts activity to involve both elementary and secondary students is the Occu-Pak Mini Course. For nine weeks, secondary students participate in the development of an occupational information package which is later used as an individualized career education tool in elementary grades. The secondary students conduct an in-depth study of a specific career and apply their communication skills to the creation of the Occu-Pak. These are some of the activities the students are asked to do during the nine-week study:

Write five sample letters of inquiry about various jobs, using correct business letter format.

Write two sample letters of appreciation for information received.

Conduct two taped interviews that are prepared with the teacher's help. Interview subjects should be able to provide information about the selected career.

Develop a list of twenty-five vocabulary words related to the selected career and define them.

Collect five to ten pictures, either snapshots or commercial productions, of the job environment or a job-related aspect.

Write a narrative description of the career field in 200–300 words and include required education and training, work conditions, and so on. Free and inexpensive brochures can be included.

Design a creative display of some kind that advertises or illustrates the career.

Design a test of general knowledge about the career, based on the information provided, for elementary school children.

Students then present their Occu-Paks to children in elementary schools. (Source: Clella J. Camp)

Language in Everyday Life

Although different careers require different knowledge, abilities, and attitudes, the ability to communicate successfully with other people enhances all careers. Top-level executives must have this skill, but it has application for every worker who deals with other workers.

By studying some basic concepts in general semantics, students become increasingly aware of the use and misuse of language and become more effective in their communication on the job. The books listed below are recommended to teachers who want to introduce students to the study of semantics. (Source: Edward V. Cornely, ed., *Integration of Career Education Concepts into the High School Curriculum.*)

Allen, Robert W., and Greene, Loren. *The Propaganda Game.* New Haven: AIM Publishers, 1969.

Chase, Stuart. *The Tyranny of Words.* New York: Harcourt, Brace and World, 1938.

Chase, Stuart. *Power of Words.* New York: Harcourt, Brace and World, 1954.

Fabun, Don. *Communication.* Beverly Hills: Glencoe Press, 1968.

Hayakawa, S. I. *Language in Thought and Action.* 3rd ed. New York: Harcourt Brace Jovanovich, 1972.

Johnson, Wendell. *People in Quandaries.* New York: Harper, 1946.

Johnson, Wendell. *Your Most Enchanted Listener.* San Francisco: International Society for General Semantics, 1956.

Korzybski, Alfred. *Science and Sanity.* New York: Harper, 1941.

Lee, Irving J. *Language Habits in Human Affairs.* New York: Harper, 1941.

Lee, Irving J. *The Language of Wisdom and Folly.* San Francisco: International Society for General Semantics, 1967.

Trade and Professional Journals

The professional or trade journals of various career fields are a rich source of career information. Ask students to obtain examples of these publications from the library, parents or friends, unions, professional associations, or community businesses. Have students search the publications for information about the profession involved, such as:

> Issues and problems of concern to individuals in the profession or trade.
>
> Current job advertisements and news articles about employment outlook.
>
> Articles about the nature and scope of the work of most persons in the field.
>
> Articles about future developments in the field or in society affecting the nature of the work involved.
>
> News items about events from the community in which the student resides, and names of organizational officers on the local or regional level.

Reading recent issues of professional and trade journals can acquaint students with issues and ideas of concern to those in various career fields, and can help them make better career decisions. (Source: Gary L. Houpt, *Strategies for Teaching English in Career Education.*)

Life, Literature, and Careers

Below is a list of short stories, poems, and books, suitable for senior high school students, that relate the stories of people in various professions. Following are some suggestions for activities that can be designed around these and similar works. (Source: Pennsylvania Curriculum Guide, Senior High Volume)

> Students can choose several of the poems, short stories, or novels that portray a particular profession, and analyze the depiction of the profession and the leading character. Students can examine how the choice of profession determined and was determined by the character's life-style; whether the depiction in literature is still relevant for today or for the near future; and the attitudes, beliefs, values, and orientation of the characters in the profession.

Students can decide on the career they hope to have and then search for literature (traditional or contemporary, fiction or poetry) in which the career is portrayed. They can utilize the reference books in the school or public library and ask for the assistance of librarians during their search. They should also visit bookstores to look for current books, and ask people currently in the profession for suggestions of books to read.

Students can share with their classmates the results of their study in an oral or written report and tell where they obtained their information, what they learned, and how they now view the profession.

Books

Anderson, Sherwood. *The Egg.* (chicken farm and small restaurant owner)

Braithwaite, E. R. *To Sir with Love.* (teacher)

Conrad, Joseph. *Heart of Darkness.* (experienced seaman)

Conrad, Joseph. *Lord Jim.* (experienced seaman)

Dreiser, Theodore. *An American Tragedy.* (attorney and business man)

Dreiser, Theodore. *Sister Carrie.* (traveling salesman)

Forster, E. M. *A Passage to India.* (surgeon, principal, and teacher)

Godey, John. *The Taking of Pelham One, Two, Three.* (transportation management)

Green, Hannah. *I Never Promised You a Rose Garden.* (psychiatrist)

Greene, Graham. *The Power and the Glory.* (priest)

Hemingway, Ernest. *The Old Man and the Sea.* (fisherman)

Kaufman, Bel. *Up the Down Staircase.* (teacher)

Keyes, Daniel. *Flowers for Algernon.* (medical profession)

Lawrence, D. H. *Sons and Lovers.* (coal miner)

Lewis, Sinclair. *Arrowsmith.* (medical researcher)

Malamud, Bernard. *The Assistant.* (small business—grocery store owner)

O'Connor, Edwin. *The Last Hurrah.* (politician)

O'Hara, John. *Appointment in Samarra.* (business executive)

Plath, Sylvia. *The Bell Jar.* (journalist and psychiatrist)

Porter, Katherine Ann. *He.* (mother)

Rand, Ayn. *The Fountainhead.* (architect)

Thurber, James. *The Secret Life of Walter Mitty.* (fantasizing about careers)

Trumbo, Dalton. *Johnny Got His Gun.* (veterans' hospital staff)

Wambaugh, Joseph. *The New Centurions.* (police officer)

Warren, Robert Penn. *All the King's Men.* (politician and director of state hospital)

Warren, Robert Penn. *The Patented Gate and the Mean Hamburger.* (running a diner)

Wells, H. G. *Tono-Bungay.* (aeronautical engineering and patent medicine)

Welty, Eudora. *A Visit of Charity.* (nursing home personnel)

Wicker, Tom. *Facing the Lions.* (newspaper publishing)

Poems

Cummings, E. E. "A Politician Is an Arse Upon."

Graves, Robert. "A Civil Servant."

Lawrence, D. H. "What Is He?" (cabinet maker)

McGough, Robert. "My Bus Conductor."

Plath, Sylvia. "Night Shift." (factory workers)

Roethke, Theodore. "Dolor." (office worker)

Sandburg, Carl. "Buyers and Sellers." (laborers, generally)

Sandburg, Carl. "Jazz Fantasies." (jazz musician)

Sandburg, Carl. "Lines Written for Gene Kelly to Dance To."

Occupational Survey Guide

Students usually need guidance when they are reading career literature or conducting research and interviewing people in regard to careers. This set of questions can be used to help them evaluate and organize their findings. (Source: Margie Brandt and Sue Merkhofer, *Career English Curriculum Guide, Phase I-II.*)

What is the nature of the occupation and what are the general duties?

What are the qualifications for employment?

What education and specialized training are required?

What is the employment outlook?

What are some methods of entering the occupation?

What are the opportunities for advancement?

What are some related occupations?

What are the typical salaries of people in this occupation?

What are the typical working conditions?

What are the advantages and disadvantages of entering this occupation?

How does the occupation relate to the students' major interests, aptitudes, abilities, values, and personal qualities?

How to Apply for a Job

Students in senior high school can prepare for seeking employment by learning how to write letters of interest and application, job resumes, job applications, and job-interview thank-you letters in their English classes. Teachers can explain the elements of the various letters and other items and actually help students to write their first formal job resumes. Samples of the students' work can be mimeographed and distributed to other students, to be used as models.

Employment interviewers from local business or industry can be invited to visit the class to evaluate the students' written assignments and to tell them what is expected of those who apply for jobs with the firms they represent. They can also bring sample forms or letters to share with students. (Source: Gary L. Houpt)

The Road Not Taken

Robert Frost's poem "The Road Not Taken" can be used to help students understand the process of making choices. Below are some questions for them to ponder, to guide their thinking. (Source: *Hawaii Career Development Continuum.*)

Why did the persona take the "road less traveled by"?

What does the persona mean by the line "And that has made all the difference"?

How does the message of this poem relate to the process of choosing one's life work? How important is it for people to choose the road (career) that seems best for them, even if they can't be sure that it is?

Understanding Company Benefits and Policies

As high school juniors and seniors prepare for jobs upon graduation, they need to be able to read and understand the job literature that they will receive upon employment. Teachers can provide students with examples of company brochures relating to health insurance and sick leave, retirement, employee credit union, on-the-job education, vacation policies, general personnel policies, union activities, and recreation and health programs sponsored by the company. English teachers can invite the teacher from the department of business to talk to their classes about some of the most common legal and technical terms found in such brochures. This activity can acquaint students with their rights and their responsibilities as employees, and provides first-hand experience in dealing with the array of company materials that are representative of most firms. (Source: *New Directions in English.* Oklahoma.)

Using the Newspaper to Identify Job Opportunities

When high school students begin their search for jobs they frequently rely on the community newspaper's want-ads section. However, because they lack work experience they sometimes have difficulty understanding the language and abbreviations used in classified advertisements. Teachers can ask students to bring in sample advertisement sections, and assist them in decoding the abbreviations used. This can lead to a discussion of the various job openings and the relative demand for workers in various fields. In addition, students can be shown how to become alert to job opportunities with new or expanding firms by reading the news sections of papers, which often have stories about openings of new businesses and other employment-related developments in the community. Students can look for clues such as when the firm will open, the projected need for employees (both number and type), the nature and location of the business, and the name of the personnel director. (Source: *New Directions in English*. Oklahoma.)

Writing for Radio

The activities suggested below provide experience in the special skills needed by writers for the medium of radio. The student is projected into an actual situation, which lends reality to the exercise. (Source: Susan Glahn and Clyde Welter)

> Pretend that you are a commercial-writer for a radio station and have been given the assignment of writing a thirty-second commercial for a pizza restaurant in your community. You must write convincingly—make listeners want to buy the pizza—and you have only thirty seconds to air the commercial. First determine whether you work for an AM or FM station, the time when the commercial is to be aired (morning, afternoon, evening), and the market for which the commercial is designed (age, income, educational level).
>
> Pretend that you are a news writer for your community radio station. Write a special news feature (one minute in length) for either the local news or sports segment. Give news about sports events or issues in the community and make your story accurate and interesting.

II Resources

4 Sources of Career Education Resources

There is an abundant literature on career education. Countless articles, books, monographs, government publications, research studies, and policy papers are available. Indeed, for those in search of such resources, the only question is where to begin. The rest of this book is designed to aid in the search, beginning here with some general suggestions and the names and addresses of various organizations and agencies that offer a variety of career education services and materials. The two remaining sections on resources deal with specific materials on career education, as it relates first to English and then to education in general.

Here, then, are some search strategies, any or all of which may be helpful in leading teachers to the multitude of sources, ranging from local to national:

> Teachers should begin their search for materials within their own departments and schools. Very often the department office, the school library, and the school guidance office can supply career education information and materials that are usable in the classroom.

> Teachers can call, write, or visit their subject supervisors or career education coordinators and resource persons in their school district's central office. Often these people have collections of career education materials and can refer teachers to others. The school district's audiovisual center may have career-related films for rental and a catalog that lists other such resources.

> Many civic, professional, and labor organizations within the local community provide publications and services related to career education.

> Regional offices of the state department of education usually can provide publications, films, consultants, and services in all educational areas.

Teachers can obtain information or materials from the state supervisor of English language arts and reading and from the state career education coordinator. Most state agencies have an extensive library of resources and often house ERIC microfiche collections. Many states have available for teachers excellent resource directories and state plans for career education, and curriculum guides for implementing career education concepts into the curricula of all subject areas. (Addresses of state departments are listed later in this section.)

Regional educational commissions representing groups of states often have career education materials and resources.

At the national level, there are numerous sources of information. The ERIC Clearinghouse System provides several kinds of user services and publications related to career education. The ERIC Clearinghouse on Adult, Career and Vocational Education at Ohio State University can be especially helpful.

The National Council of Teachers of English and its affiliates, and professional associations for educators in many other fields, have produced materials on career education. Teachers should write to the national headquarters or contact the officers of local, state, or regional affiliates.

Commercial producers of books, magazines, and newspapers have made available many kinds of materials for both students and teachers. Some of these publications for students are *Real World* (King Features Syndicate) and *Career World* (Curriculum Innovations). Teacher oriented curriculum materials for career education available from numerous publishers include curriculum guides, films, learning kits and games, and books.

The U.S. Office of Education provides many publications and services related to career education, primarily through the Office of Career Education, the National Institute of Education, and the National Advisory Council for Career Education. Other federal agencies, such as the U.S. Department of Labor, also provide excellent materials for students and teachers.

Resource Inventories

It is important for teachers to begin the search for career education publications and assistance within their schools and communities. A systematic inventory is one way of finding the resources that are close at hand. Two forms from Charles W. Ryan's *Career Education: A Handbook of Funding Resources* are included below as suggestions for making such an inventory. The first is a checklist for the teacher to use in determining the resources within the school itself; the second is a questionnaire which the teacher can send to representatives of business, industry, labor, and other appropriate groups within the community. Inventive teachers will, of course, think of other specific ways to assess the resources that are locally available for enriching their career education programs.

School Resources Inventory

	Yes	No
Media Resources		
Career Resource Center	___	___
Vocational Guidance Kits	___	___
Career Films	___	___
Career Filmstrips	___	___
Videotaping Equipment	___	___
Camera	___	___
Biographical/Autobiographical Readings	___	___
Varied Materials (costumes, posters, etc.)	___	___
Occupational Briefs	___	___
Parent Resources		
Resource File System	___	___
List of Potential Speakers	___	___
List of Career Demonstrations	___	___
Parental Aides for Field Trips	___	___
Faculty Resources		
Staff with Industrial Work Experience	___	___
Special Career Interests or Hobbies Identified	___	___
Special Course Training in Career Education	___	___
Curriculum Demonstrations in Career Areas	___	___
School Facilities		
Tools in Classrooms	___	___
Small Conference Rooms	___	___
Convertible Classrooms	___	___
Guidance Suite	___	___
Teacher Planning Areas	___	___
Library Career Resource Materials	___	___
Resource People on Local Staff	___	___
Flexible Scheduling	___	___
Curriculum Materials in Career Development	___	___
Community Resources		
Plants with 50 or More Workers	___	___
Chamber of Commerce	___	___
Rotary, Lions, Kiwanis	___	___
Speaker Bureau	___	___
Community Development Office	___	___
Employment Security Agency	___	___
School-Community Advisory Committee	___	___

Community Resources Inventory

The Career Education Advisory Committee is seeking to identify and to classify business and industry resources that could support the educational program of _____ school. The purpose of this inventory is to locate work stations, facilities, speakers, and funds to support the Career Education program.

Name: _____ Phone: _____

Address: _____ Business: _____

Description of Business: _____

_____

_____

1. What size groups could visit your Business or Plant?

    _____ (Large: 20+)   _____ (Small: 2–10)

    _____ (Medium: 10–20)   _____ (Individual: one to one)

2. Would you be willing to speak or demonstrate your occupation in the school?

    _____ Yes   _____ No

3. What funds are earmarked by your company to support local educational agencies?

    _____ ($100/year)   _____ ($1000+/year)

    _____ ($100–$500/year)   _____ (Other: _____)

    _____ ($500–$1000/year)

4. Would your firm hire part-time employees from the school?

    _____ Yes   _____ No

5. Would you be willing to explore cooperative activities with the Advisory Committee?

    _____ Yes   _____ No

6. What kinds of jobs are or may be available for beginners?

    Jobs: _____ Duties: _____

    _____

7. Are there career information materials, seminars, or on-site training opportunities in your business? Would you be willing to send these to the school?

    _____ Yes   _____ No

8. Would you be willing to participate in career development activities sponsored by the school?

    _____ Yes   _____ No

State Departments of Education

Alabama: State Department of Education, 111 Coliseum, Montgomery, AL 36109

Alaska: State Department of Education, Alaska Office Building, Pouch F, Juneau, AK 99811

Arizona: State Department of Education, 1535 W. Jefferson St., Phoenix, AZ 85007

Arkansas: State Department of Education, State Education Building, Little Rock, AR 72201

California: State Department of Education, 721 Capitol Mall, Sacramento, CA 95814

Colorado: State Department of Education, State Office Building, 201 E. Colfax Street, Denver, CO 80203

Connecticut: State Department of Education, State Office Building, Box 2219, Hartford, CT 06115

Delaware: Department of Public Instruction, John Townsend Building, Dover, DE 19901

District of Columbia: Public Schools of the District of Columbia, 415 12th St., N.W., Washington, DC 20004

Florida: Florida Department of Education, Knott Building, Tallahassee, FL 32301

Georgia: Department of Education, State Office Building, Atlanta, GA 30334

Hawaii: Department of Education, P.O. Box 2360, Honolulu, HI 96804

Idaho: State Department of Education, Len B. Jordan Office Building, Boise, ID 83720

Illinois: Illinois Office of Education, 100 N. First St., Springfield, IL 62777

Indiana: State Department of Education, State House, Rm. 229, Indianapolis, IN 46204

Iowa: Department of Public Instruction, Grimes State Office Building, Des Moines, IA 50319

Kansas: State Department of Education, 120 E. 10th St., Topeka, KS 66612

Kentucky: State Department of Education, Capitol Plaza Tower, Frankfort, KY 40601

Louisiana: State Department of Education, State Office Building, P.O. Box 44064, Capitol Station, Baton Rouge, LA 70804

Maine: Department of Educational and Cultural Services, Division of Instruction, Augusta, ME 04330

Maryland: State Department of Education, Box 8717, Baltimore, MD 21240

Massachusetts: State Department of Education, 182 Tremont St., Boston, MA 02111

Michigan: State Department of Education, P.O. Box 30008, Lansing, MI 48909

Minnesota: State Department of Education, 4th Floor, Centennial Bldg., St. Paul, MN 55101

Mississippi: State Department of Education, Sillers State Office Building, P.O. Box 771, Jackson, MS 39205

Missouri: State Department of Education, Jefferson Building, P.O. Box 480, Jefferson City, MO 65102

Montana: Office of the Superintendent of Public Instruction, State Capitol, Helena, MT 59601

Nebraska: State Department of Education, 301 Centennial Mall S., Lincoln, NE 68509

Nevada: State Department of Education, Capitol Complex, 400 W. King St., Carson City, NV 89701

New Hampshire: State Department of Education, 410 State House Annex, Concord, NH 03301

New Jersey: State Department of Education, 225 W. State St., Trenton, NJ 08625

New Mexico: State Department of Education, State Education Building, Santa Fe, NM 87501

New York: State Education Department, State Education Building, 99 Washington Ave., Albany, NY 12234

North Carolina: State Department of Public Instruction, State Education Building, Raleigh, NC 27611

North Dakota: State Department of Public Instruction, State Capitol Building, Bismarck, ND 58505

Ohio: State Department of Education, State Education Building, 65 S. Front—OH Depts. Building, Columbus, OH 43215

Oklahoma: State Department of Education, Oliver Hodge Memorial Education Building, Oklahoma City, OK 73105

Oregon: State Department of Education, 942 Lancaster Dr., N.E., Salem, OR 97310

Pennsylvania: State Department of Education, P.O. Box 911, Harrisburg, PA 17126

Rhode Island: State Department of Education, 199 Promenade St., Providence, RI 02908

South Carolina: State Department of Education, 1429 Senate St., Columbia, SC 29201

South Dakota: State Department of Education, State Office Building No. 3, Pierre, SD 57501

Tennessee: State Department of Education, 114 Cordell Hull Building, Nashville, TN 37219

Texas: Texas Education Agency, 201 E. 11th St., Austin, TX 78701

Utah: Utah Department of Public Instruction, 250 E. South Fifth St., Salt Lake City, UT 84111

Vermont: State Department of Education, Montpelier, VT 05602

Virginia: Virginia Department of Public Instruction, Box 60, Richmond, VA 23216

Washington: Office of Public Instruction, Old Capitol Building, Olympia, WA 98504

West Virginia: State Department of Education, 1900 Washington St., E., Charleston, WV 25305

Wisconsin: State Department of Public Instruction, 126 Langdon St., Madison, WI 53702

Wyoming: State Department of Education, State Office Building, West Cheyenne, WY 82002

American Samoa: Department of Education, Pago Pago, AS 96799

Canal Zone: Panama Canal Government, Schools Division, Box M, Balboa Heights, CZ

Guam: Department of Education, P.O. Box DE, Agana, GU 96910

Puerto Rico: State Department of Education, Apartado 759, Hato Rey, PR 00919

Virgin Islands: Department of Education, P.O. Box I, Christiansted, St. Croix, VI 00820

Trust Territory of the Pacific Islands: Department of Education, Saipan, Mariana Islands, TT 96950

Career Education Information Centers

There are two national centers for information on career education: the ERIC Clearinghouse on Adult, Career and Vocational Education located at Ohio State University, and the National Center for Career Education at the University of Montana. In addition, the Office of Career Education within the U.S. Office of Education provides information on career education.

ERIC Clearinghouse on Adult, Career and Vocational Education

The ERIC Clearinghouse on Adult, Career and Vocational Education is one of the primary sources of information on career education. The clearinghouse is part of ERIC (Educational Resources Information Center), a national computer-based information system which indexes articles from over 700 educational journals in the monthly catalog *Current Index to Journals in Education* (CIJE), and obtains and makes available hard-to-find, often unpublished information in the monthly catalog *Resources in Education* (RIE).

Sponsored by the National Institute of Education (NIE), the ERIC system uses a nation wide network of sixteen special-focus clearinghouses to acquire, select, annotate, and index current printed materials. The clearinghouses are usually located within established educational institutions or professional associations (the ERIC Clearinghouse on Reading and Communication Skills at NCTE is an example). A director and professional and technical staff administer each clearinghouse.

All clearinghouses in the ERIC system share three common responsibilities: processing, user services, and publication.

Processing Materials into ERIC

The staff reviews educational journals to identify articles to be included in CIJE. Articles are indexed by descriptors and arranged by subject, author, institution, and main journal citation in CIJE.

The staff also reviews hard-to-find, generally unpublished materials which are of interest to educational researchers: government documents and reports, position papers, speeches, curriculum guides, bibliographies, conference proceedings, and evaluation studies. These materials are annotated and indexed monthly in RIE by author, subject, and institution. Because these materials are difficult to find and obtain, ERIC maintains

microfiche copies, known as the ERIC collection, in major
university libraries and state education agencies. RIE and CIJE
catalogs are available wherever a collection is housed. In addition, copies of most documents are available for purchase
in either microfiche or hardcover form from ERIC Document
Reproduction Service, P.O. Box 190, Arlington, VA 22210. To
order documents, send the title and author of the document,
its ED (ERIC document) number (located in the RIE catalog),
and a check or money order.

Providing User Services

Professional and technical staffs at the clearinghouse are available to assist individuals and organizations with their search
for information. They will answer mail and telephone inquiries,
provide orientation for visitors, consult on specific user needs,
refer users to other sources of information, conduct computer
searches of ERIC and other data bases (at a nominal cost),
and give workshops on the use of ERIC and topics related to the
clearinghouse. In addition, the staff can identify ERIC microfiche
collections and computer search services in each state.

Producing Clearinghouse Publications

A clearinghouse staff prepares and commissions several types
of materials that address needs and problems of the subject of
its clearinghouse—for instance, major reports and research
papers, bibliographies, newsletters and bulletins, and special
articles for educational periodicals. Anyone can request a copy
of the clearinghouse's publications list. At some clearinghouses,
such as that for adult, career and vocational education, one
can request to be placed on the publications mailing list. Addi-
tionally, the staff welcomes suggestions for future clearinghouse
publications and invitations to contribute to educational newsletters and journals.

For more information, contact: ERIC Clearinghouse on Adult,
Career and Vocational Education, Ohio State University, 1960
Kenny Rd., Columbus, OH 43210 or call (614) 486-3655.

Office of Career Education

The Office of Career Education (OCE) within the U.S. Office
of Education is an excellent source of general information about
current career education policy, programs, and legislation. OCE

produces several documents, such as position papers, bibliographies, project descriptions, and a monograph series. Although some documents are available directly from OCE, most are eventually made available to the public by: Superintendent of Documents, U.S. Government Printing Office, Washington, DC 20402. Telephone inquiries can be made by calling (202) 245-2331, and mail inquiries can be addressed to: Office of Career Education, Room 3108, ROB #3, 7th and D St., SW, Washington, DC 20202.

The National Center for Career Education

The National Center for Career Education is a center for the collection and dissemination of instructional materials in career education, suitable for classroom use. The Center's goals are to provide lists of instructional materials in the various subject areas, to conduct computer searches of materials, and to make available sample materials, or "mini-libraries," for classroom use. For more information, write: National Center for Career Education, University of Montana, P.O. Box 7815, Missoula, MT 59807 or call (406) 243-5262/6466.

National Career Information Center

Sponsored by the American Personnel and Guidance Association (APGA), the National Career Information Center (NCIC) is involved in the identification, evaluation, and utilization of career information for counselors and others involved in education. The services of the NCIC involve collecting, evaluating, and disseminating information on career education materials and communicating effective approaches for providing career guidance. Publications and products of APGA and NCIC that may be of interest to educators are listed below and are available from: American Personnel and Guidance Association, 2 Skyline Place—Suite 400, 5203 Leesburg Pike, Falls Church, VA 22041.

Inform—a monthly newsletter identifying accurate, relevant, career information sources and innovative techniques for guidance.

Career Resource Bibliographies—twenty bibliographies of career information for various career cluster areas ($0.75 each).

Counseling Resources—yearly catalog of over 100 books and 100 films for purchase or rental, suitable for career education and career guidance in schools.

Career Education Publications

Various newsletters and other periodicals are issued by a number of organizations engaged in career education. Teachers may write the sponsoring agency for subscription information and answers to questions concerning content and suitability for classroom use.

Newsletters

Career Education News. Bobit Publishing Company, 1155 Waukegan Rd., Glenview, IL 60025

Career Education in the States. Task Force on Career Education of the Education Commission on the States, 1860 Lincoln St. —Suite 300, Denver, CO 80295

Career Education Workshop. Parker Publishing Company, Route 59A at Brookhill Dr., West Nyack, NY 10994

CES News. 875 N. Michigan Ave.—Suite 1850, Chicago, IL 60611

Education and Work. Capitol Publishing Company, 2430 Pennsylvania Ave.—Suite G12, Washington, DC 20037

ERIC Clipboard. ERIC Clearinghouse on Adult, Career and Vocational Education, Ohio State University, 1960 Kenny Rd., Columbus, OH 43210

Inform. National Career Information Center, American Personnel and Guidance Association, 2 Skyline Place—Suite 400, 5203 Leesburg Pike, Falls Church, VA 22041

Manpower and Vocational Education Weekly. Capitol Publishing Company, 2430 Pennsylvania Ave.—Suite G12, Washington, DC 20037

News from NACE. National Association for Career Education, c/o Office of Career Education, Glassboro State College, Glassboro, NJ 08028

Other Periodicals

Career Education Quarterly. National Association of Career Education, c/o Boston University, School of Education, 765 Commonwealth Ave.—Rm. 1502, Boston, MA 02215

Journal of Career Education. University of Missouri—Columbia, College of Education, Rm. 111 Education Building, Columbia, MO 65211

Interested Professional Associations

Career information of general interest to all teachers is obtainable from these organizations. The National Association for Career Education is a professional association for career educators at all levels. Besides issuing newsletters and other publications it answers specific questions about career education developments in the various states. The National Association for Industry—Education Cooperation is a collaborative effort by schools and industry to supply information regarding events and activities of mutual interest to members in both fields. It publishes a newsletter, pamphlets, and other career literature.

National Association for Career Education, Glassboro State College, Glassboro, NJ 08028

National Association for Industry-Education Cooperation, 235 Hendricks Blvd., Buffalo, NY 14226

Professional Assocations for English Educators

Educational materials related to careers in the language arts, as well as in the various forms of communication, are available from the following professional organizations for English educators. These materials include pamphlets, books, curriculum and teaching guides, and other resources. Publications catalogs also are available.

International Reading Association, 800 Barksdale Rd., Newark, DE 19711

Modern Language Association, 52 Fifth Ave., New York, NY 10011

National Council of Teachers of English (and the ERIC Clearinghouse on Reading and Communication Skills), 1111 Kenyon Rd., Urbana, IL 61801

Speech Communication Association, 5205 Leesburg Pike—Suite 1001, Falls Church, VA 22041

Professional Associations in Communication

Materials related specifically to careers in the various aspects and media of communications are available from numerous professional associations. Following are some that should be good sources of career information for students and teachers.

American Advertising Federation, 1225 Connecticut Ave., NW, Washington, DC 20036

American Business Communications Association, 911 S. Sixth St., Champaign, IL 61820

American Federation of Television and Radio Artists, 1350 Sixth Ave., New York, NY 10019

American Library Association, 50 E. Huron St., Chicago, IL 60611

American Newspaper Publishers Association Foundation, The Newspaper Center, Box 17407, Washington, DC 20041

American Women in Radio and Television, 1321 Connecticut Ave., NW, Washington, DC 20036

Association of American Publishers, Inc., 1 Park Ave., New York, NY 10016

Magazine Publishers Association, Inc., 575 Lexington Ave., New York, NY 10022

National Association of Broadcasters, 1771 N. St., NW, Washington, DC 20036

National Writer's Club, 1450 S. Havana St.—Suite 620, Aurora, CO 80012

Society for Technical Communication, 1010 Vermont Ave., NW, Washington, DC 20005

Women in Communication, Box 9561, Austin, TX 78766

Federal Sources of Information

Agencies

Department of Health, Education and Welfare, 200 Independence Ave., SW, Washington, DC 20201

National Center for Education Statistics, Adult and Vocational Education Survey Branch, Room 3071, 400 Maryland Ave., SW, Washington, DC 20202

National Institute of Education, Brown Bldg., 19th and M Sts., NW, Washington, DC 20208

U.S. Office of Education, 400 Maryland Ave., SW, Washington, DC 20202

Bureau of Occupational and Adult Education, U.S. Office of Education, Room 4153, 400 Maryland Ave., SW, Washington, DC 20202

Office of Career Education, U.S. Office of Education, Room 3108, ROB #3, 7th and D Sts., SW, Washington, DC 20202

Department of Labor, Room S 1032, Information Office, 200 Constitution Ave., NW, Washington, DC 20210

Bureau of Labor Statistics, Department of Labor, Room 1539, General Accounting Office Bldg., 441 G St., NW, Washington, DC 20212

Employment and Training Administration, Department of Labor, Room 10255, 601 D St., NW, Washington, DC 20213

Women's Bureau, Department of Labor, Office of the Secretary, 200 Constitution Ave., NW, Washington, DC 20210

Publications and Services Distribution

Superintendent of Documents, U.S. Government Printing Office, Washington, DC 20402; Public Inquiry Number: (202) 783-3238 for information about prices, titles, authors.

ERIC Document Reproduction Services, P.O. Box 190, Arlington, VA 22210

National Audio Visual Center, National Archives and Records Service, General Services Administration, Washington, DC 20409; Request catalog *Career Education: Selected U.S. Government Audiovisuals* for titles, purchase and rental plans of items from more than 150 government agencies.

5 Career Education and English Resources

Following are a number of useful bibliographies of career education and English materials. They can provide access to the whole range of interests and possibilities explored in the career education literature related to English and the language arts. Noteworthy articles and books are identified and annotated on subsequent pages.

American Personnel and Guidance Association. *Careers in Communications and Media.* Falls Church, Va.: National Career Information Center Resource Bibliography, vol. 5, no. 1 (1976).

Donelson, Kenneth L., ed. *Books for You: A Booklist for Senior High Students.* Urbana, Ill.: National Council of Teachers of English, 1976 (pp. 121–130).

Hansen, Mary Lewis, et al. *A Preliminary Exploration of Occupations in the Arts and Humanities.* Cambridge, Mass.: Technical Education Research Center, 1975. Arlington, Va.: ERIC Document Reproduction Service, ED 137 611.

Kennedy, Elsie. *Exploring Careers in Fine Arts and Humanities: A Guide for Teachers.* Lexington: Curriculum Development Center, Education Building, University of Kentucky, 1974. Arlington, Va.: ERIC Document Reproduction Service, ED 098 416.

Loheyde, Kathy. *Annotated Bibliography of Career-Relevant Literature at the Junior and Senior High School Level.* Ithaca, N.Y.: Instructional Materials Service, Cornell Institute for Research and Development in Occupational Education, Cornell University, December 1972. Arlington, Va.: ERIC Document Reproduction Service, ED 076 830.

Ritvo, Phyllis T., ed. *An Annotated Bibliography of Selected Curriculum Materials in the Arts and Humanities.* Cambridge, Mass.: Technical Education Research Center, 1975. Arlington, Va.: ERIC Document Reproduction Service, ED 137 606.

Articles

Davidson, Dorothy; Dougherty, Mildred; Perry, Jesse; Yesner, Seymour; and Farmer, Marjorie. "Career Education in the English Classroom." In *Career Education in the Academic Classroom,* pp. 57–73. Eds. Garth L. Mangum, James W. Becker, Garn Coombs, and Pat Marshall. Salt Lake City: Olympus, 1975.

One of several papers presented at a conference on career education for classroom teachers from national associations representing seven academic areas, sponsored by the National Foundation for the Improvement of Education. This essay reflects the discussion and concerns of those who represented the National Council of Teachers of English and is one of the early, seminal works on the topic. The authors examine the historical purposes of English studies and how they relate to the goals of career education. They describe strategies and sample exercises for integrating four career education goals into the K–12 English curriculum.

Davis, James S.; and Nall, Roger. "English and Career Education: A Re-Vision of Resources." *English Education* 10 (December 1978): 96–101.

The authors assert that integrating career education concepts into the English curriculum implies that English professionals not only help students develop effective communication skills, but also help them understand the nature and meaning of leisure and work. They discuss how books such as Richard Bolles's *What Color Is Your Parachute?,* Studs Terkel's *Working,* and Eliot Wigginton's *Moments: The Foxfire Experience* can be used to increase students' awareness of themselves and the world of work. Three sample activity-oriented activities and curriculum resources are described.

Drumsta, Michael; and Skiersch, Nancy. "Career Communication." In *A Guide for Teaching Speech Today: Six Alternative Approaches,* pp. 1–42. Ed. Mina Gail Halliday. Skokie, Ill.: National Textbook Company, 1979.

Describes a one-semester Career Communications course to assist all high school students in the development of skills needed by all people in their careers. Provides students with opportunities to examine their abilities as communicators, to explore the communication environment of various careers, and to identify careers of interest to them. Ten sample teaching units are described which focus on topics such as listening, telecommunications, interpersonal communication, and interviewing. Provides ideas for use in a speech communication unit within an English course or in the separate speech course. An excellent bibliography is included.

English Language Arts Bulletin 20 (Spring 1979). Career Education and Language Arts Issue. Ohio Council of Teachers of English Language Arts. ERIC Document Reproduction Service, Arlington, Va. (ED 172 225).

Provides several articles relating to career education and English for secondary and postsecondary teachers: "To Careers Via the English Class," "Career Alternatives for College English Majors," "From Literature Ph.D. to Communications Skills Specialist," and "Balanced Curriculum or Trojan Horse: Thoughts on Career Education and English."

Finn, Peter. "Career Education: An English/Social Studies Resource." *Media and Methods* 11 (April 1975): 20–23.

Offers teaching ideas for social studies and English teachers who want to know how to integrate career education concepts into their K–12 curriculum. Finn, a prolific writer about career education, asserts that integrating career education gives teachers the chance to introduce students to the many occupations in which language arts and social studies skills are essential, while increasing the relevance of the study of the subject-matter itself. He describes specific methods and materials for several classroom activities for social studies and English classrooms.

Gebhardt, Richard. "Balanced Curriculum or Trojan Horse: Thoughts on Career Education and English." *English Language Arts Bulletin* 20 (Spring 1979): 24–28. Ohio Council of Teachers of English Language Arts.

Examines the close relationship and compatibility of the goals of English studies and of career education. Describes how the study of English provides students with excellent preparation for career entry and advancement, and briefly surveys recent studies and books that support this belief. The author also discusses initial teacher resistance to vocationally oriented conceptions and definitions of career education in the early 1970s, and concludes that career education can and should be provided in a balanced curriculum in the English language arts.

Kaiser, Marjorie M. "Unintended Career Education in the English Classroom." *Journal of Career Education* 3 (Spring 1977): 14–24.

Reports results of the author's dissertation study of attitudes toward work that are expressed in eighth grade literature. She asserts that although the term is relatively new, the concept of career education has always been a part of the school curriculum. She shows how six anthologies unintentionally engage in career education: (1) how they illustrate the concept of work and its relation to theme and characterization; (2) the racial and sexual representations of working characters; (3) attitudes expressed toward work, work values, and the concept of occupational choice; and (4) the degree of reinforcement of ten selected career education concepts. Kaiser concludes that the inadvertent study of career education concepts is inherent in the study of literature.

Kaiser, Marjorie M. "English and Career Education." *Virginia English Bulletin* 27 (Spring 1977): 39–43. Virginia Association of Teachers of English.

A review of thirteen career education activities for the English classroom, suggested by individual teachers and authors of articles and books. Includes ideas for relating career education to the study of vocabulary, the newspaper, technical writing, television study, composition, values clarification, creative dramatics, and literature.

Kaiser, Marjorie M. "Language Arts and Career Education for the Middle and Junior High School." *Language Arts* 55 (March 1978): 302–307.

Discusses career education activities for the English language arts classroom to assist students in career exploration, helping them to see the relationship of language to work in general, to specific career clusters, and to individual jobs. Sample career education activities are described, dealing with the etymology of the vocabulary or jargon of various professions, the literature of career education and career guidance, occupational titles, word changes and inventions, and the language of work as used on television, in the names of occupations, and in adolescent literature. A resource bibliography is included.

Kaiser, Marjorie M. "The Young Adult Novel and Career Education: Another Kind of Relevance." In *Essays on Career Education and English, K-12.* Ed. Marjorie M. Kaiser. Urbana, Ill.:
National Council of Teachers of English, 1980.

Describes the many ways in which teachers can help students
identify career education concepts in the study of literature
and lists ten such concepts with an excellent bibliography that
illustrates them. Concludes with a discussion of issues and
methods in teaching young adult fiction and provides a strong
rationale for including it in the English program.

Kilby, Jan E. "Career Education: Implications for Teachers
of English." *English Education* 7 (Summer 1976): 249–251.

Defines two important responsibilities for English educators
at all levels who want to integrate career education concepts
into the teaching of English: helping students understand the
value of effective communication skills for all careers and
acquainting them with the many opportunities for employment
within the communication career cluster. Includes a list of
eight guidelines for action for teachers who want to develop
career education programs.

Kingsbury, Mary. "The World of Work in Children's Fiction."
Language Arts 52 (October 1975): 972–975, 1018.

Reports results of the author's research into the degree to
which career education concepts and work values are presented
to children in ninety-one realistic fiction books of the 1930s,
1950s, and 1970s. Statistics relating to occupations are analyzed and evaluated in light of how work roles, attitudes, and
values are portrayed by various characters in several books.
Kingsbury concludes that children's fiction presents only a
partial view of the world of work and its rewards; that it
values women in certain occupations but bars them from
others; that it often questions the traditional work ethic; and
that it lacks a variety of work models for children.

The Leaflet 74 (Fall 1975). Double Issue on Vocational Education.
New England Association of Teachers of English.

An early effort to assess the interests and concerns of English
professionals in career and vocational education. Published
as a result of a national call for manuscripts on the subject,
the seventeen essays clarify the emerging concept of career

education and present diverse views on various aspects of English and vocational education.

LeBlanc, Robert; and Mountain, Lee. "To Careers Via the English Class." *English Language Arts Bulletin* 20 (Spring 1979): 1–7. Ohio Council of Teachers of English Language Arts.

Describes a model career education unit which can easily be used in an English classroom. Includes several introductory activities to acquaint students with the concept of career clusters, with twenty activities to help students understand the reading and writing requirements of each cluster, and several follow-up activities relating to job applications, resumes, and interviews to help students learn how to make individual career choices.

McLeod, Alan. "Stimulating Writing through Job Awareness." *English Journal* 67 (November 1978): 42–43.

Reports results of a career education inservice program for classroom teachers and guidance counselors to identify what the business community expects of prospective employees, what community resources are available for instruction in secondary schools, and what secondary teachers can do to enhance students' job success. Data were collected during on-site visits to community organizations and businesses. Significant discoveries about people and the world of work emerged. Presents a list of thirty-four oral and written career education activities intended especially to stimulate student writing.

Marland, Sidney P. "Meeting Our Enemies: Career Education and the Humanities." *English Journal* 21 (September 1973): 900–906.

Focuses on the relationship between career education and the humanities and the concept of career education as an "instructional strategy" to relate teaching and learning to career development. Discusses career clusters and gives examples of classroom methods for acquainting students with them. Reviews the long history of the liberal arts tradition with its early emphasis on occupational orientation, preparing students for careers in the church, government, and law. Marland reaffirms the importance and centrality of work in peoples' lives and asserts that "work is humanity" because it can provide intellectual and personal fulfillment.

Mitchell, Joyce Slayton. "Classroom Strategies: Integrating Strategies for English-related Careers." In *The Classroom Teacher's Workbook for Career Education,* pp. 80–90. New York: Avon Books, 1979.

Presents specific teaching ideas for integrating career education into the K–12 English curriculum. The author suggests methods and specific materials such as poems, short stories, novels, newspapers, and magazines, which can be used to show students the many career opportunities related to the study of English.

Olsen, Henry D.; and Mangieri, John N. "Career Education in the Elementary English Curriculum." *Elementary English* 52 (January 1975): 19–22.

Discusses the importance of facilitating elementary students' career awareness in the English language arts curriculum and of acquainting them with the fifteen career clusters. A bibliography of books relating to each cluster is presented. The authors suggest that greater emphasis on career awareness can assist educators in achieving an end to sex-stereotyped occupational roles, introducing progressively more mature literature, and increasing individualized reading activities to meet students' interests and needs.

Parish, Janelle A. "Occupations in Children's Realistic Fiction." *English in Texas* 9 (Winter 1978): 40–41. Texas Council of Teachers of English.

Examines the role of educators in providing students with experiences and curriculum materials to learn about the importance of work; and reports results of a content analysis of 150 realistic fiction books for adolescents published in the 1950s and 1970s to determine whether fiction conveys a realistic view of the work world. Career types and role models are identified and worker characteristics, attitudes, and stereotypes are analyzed. The author concludes that fiction for youthful readers presents a narrow and limited view of the world of work, discriminates against women as workers, overemphasizes professional and managerial jobs at the expense of jobs involving manual labor, and does not keep pace with the complexities of today's economic and social realities.

Roberts, Richard E. "Career Investigation and Planning in the High School English Curriculum." *English Journal* 66 (November 1977): 49–52.

Describes an unusual and successful senior elective course in Career English, developed and taught by the author at Arlington Senior High School in Poughkeepsie, New York, which provides students with opportunities for career investigation and planning through a broad range of reading, writing, and research activities. Describes a typical activity involving the reading of biographical articles and books to expose students to the philosophy and psychology of work. Other units include intensive analysis of students' personalities, needs, and aspirations; the world of work and its realities; and strategies for career decision-making. The author concludes with comments about evaluation of students' progress. There are outlines of the six units and lists of books to be used in them.

Stanwood, Les. "Careers Research: Out of the Term Paper Rut." *Media and Methods* 15 (November 1978): 40–42.

Discusses a technique for having students in English classes conduct research into careers of interest to them. Students conduct library research, interview professionals in various careers, and write a term paper. The papers are evaluated and the best are placed in a Careers Guidebook in the school library for other students to read. Stanwood gives his step-by-step plan for this unit and describes its advantages over the traditional term paper approach.

Suhor, Charles. "Career Education and English: A Matter of Definition." *English Education* 5 (October/November 1973): 21–25.

Reviews popular definitions of career education and urges teachers of English to accept a far broader concept based on students' cognitive and language development. The author asserts that career education should facilitate the development of students' thinking abilities in all problem-solving situations, and not concentrate solely on specific job-related concerns.

Suhor, Charles. "Goals of Career Education and Goals of Subject-Area Instruction." *Journal of Career Education* 5 (March 1979): 215–219.

Examines the goals of career education and those of subject areas and proposes an original model to illustrate the degree to which goals relate to each other. The author concludes that not every goal of a subject area need be directly career related but that a well balanced program in any subject would be strong on congruent goals—reflecting a double orientation on both cognitive and career development—while being rich in overlapping goals and selective in distinctive goals.

Thetford, Mary. "The Case for the Career Book in Grades 5-8: A Feminist View." *Elementary English* 50 (October 1973): 1059-60, 1074.

Analyzes the fiction typically available to intermediate and junior high school students and concludes that it often contains sex-role stereotyping which can limit the goals and aspirations of students, especially young girls. Discusses the concerns of individuals and associations concerned about sex bias in fiction, and presents five questions for classroom teachers or librarians to ask in examining their materials.

Books and Booklets

Berry, Elizabeth. *The Careers of English Majors.* Urbana, Ill.: National Council of Teachers of English, 1966 (out of print); Arlington, Va.: ERIC Document Reproduction Service, ED 019 256.

Written by the chair of the NCTE Committee on Careers in English 1961-1963, this is the report of a 1962 follow-up study of the career patterns of 267 college English majors who received A.B. degrees from five midwestern liberal arts institutions during 1952-1957. Data collection techniques consisted of a standardized survey of all graduates and personal interviews with twenty-five graduates. The author describes their career patterns and attitudes in an attempt to analyze the value of the English major in the lives and careers of the graduates. The study is dated, contains uneven data analysis of women's career patterns, and relies on a rather small sample of students and institutions, but it reaffirms the value of the English major for life and career preparation.

Bestor, Dorothy Koch. *Aside from Teaching English, What in the World Can You Do?* Seattle: University of Washington Press, 1977.

An excellent career education handbook for prospective, current, and former English majors. The book is based on Bestor's perspective as a college English teacher, free-lance editor, and placement center counselor, and reflects attempts to collect data on job prospects for English majors from over 350 employers and job seekers. This handbook provides up-to-date information for English majors who want to know how their academic preparation qualifies them for a multitude of jobs in education, writing and editing, research, government service, communication and other areas. It provides names and addresses of helpful individuals and associations, bibliographical information, and other sources of career guidance, and suggestions for attaining employment. Advice is based on sound analysis of higher education and the economic realities of the current labor market.

Brod, Richard I.; Cowan, Elizabeth; and Woodruff, Neal, eds. *English and Foreign Languages: Employment and the Professions.* Joint Issue of the Association of Departments of English and Association of Departments of Foreign Languages bulletins. New York: Modern Language Association, 1976.

This collection of essays from senior scholars and from junior members of the profession focuses on philosophical and practical aspects of employment for English and foreign language majors.

Kaiser, Marjorie M., ed. *Essays on Career Education and English, K-12.* Urbana, Ill.: National Council of Teachers of English, 1980.

A collection of essays by teachers, supervisors, and administrators in English programs, by English educators, and by professionals in the community. The focus is on three themes: professional concerns relating to career education and English, broad curriculum issues, and strategies for implementing career education. The essays represent the diversity and extent of the interest of English professionals in career education.

McBath, James H.; and Burhans, David T., Jr., eds. *Communication Education for Careers.* ERIC Clearinghouse on Reading and Communication Skills Speech Communication Association Module. Falls Church, Va.: Speech Communication Association, 1975.

The authors analyze current efforts to prepare communication majors for both academic and nonacademic employment and to make recommendations regarding curricula for future programs. They describe specific learning experiences and activities to ensure that students have opportunities to develop the speech communication skills necessary to prepare them for career entry and advancement. An excellent bibliography of resources is included.

Nielsen, Duane M.; and Hjelm, Howard F., eds. *Reading and Career Education*. Newark, Del.: International Reading Association, 1975. Arlington, Va.: ERIC Document Reproduction Service, ED 104 435.

A collection of fifteen papers that were presented at a preconvention conference on reading and career education. Educators from various fields and levels comment on the importance of reading skills in all career education efforts and describe national issues, reading competencies required for careers, and exemplary career education programs.

Olson, Paul A. *The Liberal Arts and Career Education: A Look at the Past and the Future*. Monograph on Career Education. Washington, D.C.: Government Printing Office, 1975. GPO SN 017-080-01744-0 ($1.30). Arlington, Va.: ERIC Document Reproduction Service, ED 113 487.

Provides a historical perspective of the role traditionally played by the liberal arts in preparing individuals for careers and examines its role in the future. Olson asserts that the goals of liberal arts are very compatible with goals of career education and provides evidence of career orientation of the liberal arts curriculum from the twelfth century to the present. He concludes with five educational policy recommendations to continue the integration of career education concepts into the liberal arts curricula of colleges and universities.

Orange, Linwood E. *English: The Preprofessional Major*. 3rd ed. rev. New York: Modern Language Association, 1979. (Also distributed by NCTE.)

This thirty-one page pamphlet, now known as the "Orange Report," presents the results of research into the value of the English major as preparation for the professions. Since 1969, Orange has collected data from law schools, medical schools, industrial organizations, government agencies, and English majors themselves. His data reconfirm the value of the English major to both employee and employer. Orange describes the competencies developed by the study of English and demonstrates how these abilities prepare one for career entry and advancement. He concludes with practical advice for English majors and offers twenty-eight brief descriptions of entry level jobs of interest to them.

Rutan, Patricia McGeehan; and Wilson, Jeanne Turner. *Career Education and English.* Guidance Monograph Series, No. IX. Career Education and the Curriculum. Boston: Houghton Mifflin, 1975.

Focuses on the important role of the language arts curriculum in career education. Examines the history and development of the English curriculum in the United States, explores future trends in education and business, and discusses educational implications. The unique role of the language arts teacher is described, and there are three sample teaching units, a resource guide, and a bibliography.

Stewart, Charles J. *Teaching Interviewing for Career Preparation.* (Theory into Practice Series) Falls Church, Va.: Speech Communication Association, 1976.

A thirty-four page booklet to aid high school and college instructors in designing and teaching units or courses in the fundamentals of informational and employment interviewing. Theory and practice are discussed and twenty-six classroom activities are suggested. A bibliography is included.

"Newspaper in Education" Publications

Items listed below are available from American Newspaper Publishers Association Foundation, The Newspaper Center, Box 17407, Dulles International Airport, Washington, DC 20041.

Brochures

Newspaper Jobs for Journalism Grads. Single copy free; $15.00 per 100 copies.

Newspaper Jobs You Never Thought of ... Or Did You? Paul Swensson, 1976.

Newspapers ... Your Future?

NIE Teaching Materials Brochure (publications list). $5.00 per 100 copies.

Books and Pamphlets

The Anatomy of a Newspaper. Kathryn McAuley, 1975. 1–5 copies, $2.00; 6–20 copies, $1.50; 21 or more, $1.00.

Bibliography: Newspaper in Education Publications, 2nd ed. Single copy free; multiple copies $0.50.

Dateline: The World. A Guide for Using Newspapers in Language Arts and Social Studies. Secondary ed. Nancy Sparks, 1977. $3.50.

Facts about Newspapers. April 1979. Minimum order, 25 copies. $3.00.

Innovate: A Generative Guide to Inquiry Teaching of Communication Skills. Rev. ed. 1974. $3.00.

A Look at Local Culture: Humanities with the Newspaper. Ron Lindsey. $2.00.

The Newspaper in the American History Classroom. Richard F. Newton and Peter F. Sprague, 1974. $2.00.

The Newspaper in Education Introductory Kit. 1979. $1.50.

The Newspaper as an Effective Teaching Tool. 1977.

Speaking of a Free Press: A Collection of Notable Quotations about Newspapers and a Free Press. 1974. Single copy free; multiple copies $0.40 each.

Teaching Reading Skills through the Newspaper. Arnold B. Cheyney, 1971. (International Reading Association, 800 Barksdale Rd., Newark, DE 19711.) $2.00.

Using Newspapers to Teach Reading Skills. Robert M. Wilson and Marcia M. Barnes, 1975. $1.00.

Your Future in Daily Newspapers. 1979. Single copies free; multiple copies $0.60 each.

Arts and Humanities Career Series

The following publications are from the U.S. Government series "Career Exploration in the Arts and Humanities: A Series of Books for Students, Teachers and Counselors." They are available from either the U.S. Government Printing Office or ERIC Document Reproduction Service, at the addresses shown below. Prices quoted are subject to change.

Superintendent of Documents, U.S. Government Printing Office, Washington, DC 20402

ERIC Document Reproduction Service, P.O. Box 190, Arlington, VA 22210

Materials for Teachers and Counselors

Andrews, Ellen, et al. *Exploring Arts and Humanities Careers in the Community: A Program Planning Guide*. Washington, D.C.: Government Printing Office, 1976. GPO SN 017-080-01648-6 ($1.25). Arlington, Va.: ERIC Document Reproduction Service, ED 137 608.

Hansen, Mary Lewis, et al. *Three Hundred Ninety-One Ways to Explore Arts and Humanities Careers: Classroom Activities in Dance, Music, Theater and Media, Visual Arts and Crafts, Writing and Humanities*. Washington, D.C.: Government Printing Office, 1976. GPO SN 017-080-01643-5 ($2.40). Arlington, Va.: ERIC Document Reproduction Service, ED 137 607.

Ritvo, Phyllis; and Hansen, Mary Lewis. *Career Guidance in the Arts and Humanities: Activities, Information and Resources for Grades 7–12*. Washington, D.C.: Government Printing Office, 1976. GPO SN 017-080-01644-3 ($2.60). Arlington, Va.: ERIC Document Reproduction Service, ED 138 029.

Materials for Students

Allosso, Michael; and Hansen, Mary Lewis. *Exploring Theater and Media Careers: A Student Guidebook*. Washington, D.C.: Government Printing Office, 1976. GPO SN 017-080-01640-1 ($2.15). Arlington, Va.: ERIC Document Reproduction Service, ED 137 613.

Cornell, Richard; and Hansen, Mary Lewis. *Exploring Dance Careers: A Student Guidebook*. Washington, D.C.: Government Printing Office, 1976. GPO SN 017-080-01638-9 ($0.75). Arlington, Va.: ERIC Document Reproduction Service, ED 137 614.

Cornell, Richard; and Hansen, Mary Lewis. *Exploring Music Careers: A Student Guidebook*. Washington, D.C.: Government Printing Office, 1976. GPO SN 017-080-01639-7 ($1.30). Arlington, Va.: ERIC Document Reproduction Service, ED 137 615.

Dubman, Sheila; and Hansen, Mary Lewis. *Exploring Visual Arts and Crafts Careers: A Student Guidebook*. Washington, D.C.: Government Printing Office, 1976. GPO SN 017-080-

01641-9 ($2.35). Arlington, Va.: ERIC Document Reproduction Service, ED 137 609.

Hansen, Mary Lewis. *Exploring Writing Careers: A Student Guidebook.* Washington, D.C.: Government Printing Office, 1976. GPO SN 017-080-01642-7 ($1.40). Arlington, Va.: ERIC Document Reproduction Service, ED 137 612.

Workman, Jean; and Hansen, Mary Lewis. *Exploring Careers in the Humanities: A Student Guidebook.* Washington, D.C.: Government Printing Office, 1976. GPO SN 017-080-01649-4 ($2.45). Arlington, Va.: ERIC Document Reproduction Service, ED 137 610.

Curriculum Guides

Following is a list of exemplary curriculum guides from school districts or state departments of education that can be used to assist teachers of English in integrating career ecucation concepts in the K–12 English language arts curriculum. Each guide contains teaching ideas and resources, many of which have been presented in this book. The guides are useful for a number of reasons:

Most of the guides are nonspecific in regard to textbooks. They contain methods and materials that can be used in any classroom regardless of the school or district curriculum guide or textbooks.

Most guides have been developed by experienced teachers of English in collaboration with guidance specialists, curriculum developers or specialists, librarians, and other educators. They reflect a good understanding of the goals of English instruction and of the goals of career education, and sound principles of curriculum and program development.

Many of the guides contain methods and materials for various grade levels, K–12, and include activities for the study of language, literature, and composition and the development of the communication skills of reading, writing, speaking, and listening.

Many of the guides contain basic information about the concept of career education and its relation to the teaching of English. They frequently include extensive bibliography and lists of curriculum resources such as articles, books, monographs, government documents, curriculum guides, films, learning games and kits, and the names and addresses of publishers and associations providing career education materials.

These guides are available for reading or purchase through a variety of sources. First, teachers can generally obtain copies, which often are free or inexpensive, by calling or writing their school district, state language arts supervisor, their state career education coordinator, or the director of publications within their state education department (the addresses are given in the citation for each guide). Second, many of the guides have been selected for inclusion in the ERIC system and can be purchased in either microfiche or hardcover form from the ERIC Document Reproduction Service, or they can be read in microfiche form in institutions and state agencies that house ERIC collections.

Teachers can obtain copies of guides published in their own or in other states. In this way, they can acquire a wealth of information from many guides.

The guides have generally been published as a result of school district in-service programs, state or federally funded career education projects, through the efforts of the state career education advisory council or career education coordinator, or as a collaborative effort between schools and community associations. Most are available from state departments of education or educational research centers or laboratories, and those with ED numbers are obtainable from the ERIC system: ERIC Document Reproduction Service, P.O. Box 190, Arlington, VA 22210. Prices are listed in *Resources in Education* (*RIE* catalogs), for both microfiche and hardcover, and are subject to change. If the purchaser lacks access to the RIE catalog, price information is available from ERIC (state name of author or editor, title, and date of publication).

Arizona

Hindman, Helen S.; and Triem, Marion L. *Career Education in Junior High English.* Northwest Area Career Guidance Service Center, Cross Junior High, 1000 W. Chapala Dr., Tucson, AZ 85704.

Kucinski, Sharon, ed. *Activity Idea Bank.* Tucson: Flowing Wells Public Schools, 1977. ($3.00) Available from Dr. John Komar,

Arizona Department of Education, 1535 W. Jefferson St., Phoenix, AZ 85007.

Arkansas

Clark, Dorothy; Crawford, Deborah; LaGrossa, Jeanne; Matthis, Estelle; Miller, Jennalea; Muench, Betty; Warner, Velma; and Burk, Rosemary. *Just around the Corner: Career Awareness: A Guide for Elementary Teachers, 3-7.* Supervisor for Career Education, Arkansas Department of Education, State Education Bldg., Little Rock, AR 72201.

Clark, Dorothy. *And What Are You Planning to Be When You Grow Up? Career Awareness: A Guide for Elementary Teachers, K-4.* Supervisor for Career Education, Arkansas Department of Education, State Education Bldg., Little Rock, AR 72201.

Muench, Betty; Paxton, Lera; and Miller, Jennalea. *Career Education: Concepts and Bulletin Board Ideas.* (Free) Supervisor for Career Education, Arkansas Department of Education, State Education Bldg., Little Rock, AR 72201.

California

Gilliland, Katie E.; and Jehl, Jeanne. *A Career Education Unit for Junior High School: Careers for Good Speakers: Communications and Media Cluster.* 1976. ($0.60) San Diego City Schools, Materials Development Office, Room 2002, Education Center, 4100 Normal St., San Diego, CA 92103 (Stock no. 41-C-1005).

Hill, Douglas A.; and Johnson, Yvonne. *Career Education in the Elementary Grades.* 1972. ($3.00) San Diego City Schools, Materials Development Office, Room 2002, Education Center, 4100 Normal St., San Diego, CA 92103 (Stock no. 41-C-1705).

Implementing Career Education: Resources Guide. 1979. ($0.85) Publications Sales, California State Department of Education, P.O. Box 271, Sacramento, CA 95802.

Sources of Information on Career Education: An Annotated Bibliography. 1975. Publications Sales, California State Department of Education, P.O. Box 271, Sacramento, CA 95802.

Colorado

Glahn, Susan; and Welter, Clyde. *BO-CEC English Resource Guide.* (Business and Office Career Education Curriculum

Guides Series) 1975. Department of Vocational-Technical Education, Colorado State University, Ft. Collins, CO 80521. ERIC Document Reproduction Service, Arlington, Va. (ED 112 080).

Delaware

Houpt, Gary L. *Strategies for Teaching English in Career Education.* 1971. State Department of Public Instruction, Townsend Bldg., P.O. Box 1402, Dover, DE 19901. ERIC Document Reproduction Service, Arlington, Va. (ED 059-404).

Florida

Brandt, Margie; and Merkhofer, Sue. *Career English Curriculum Guide, Phase I-II.* June 1977. Career Education Office, School Board of Broward County, 1001 Northwest Fourth St., Ft. Lauderdale, FL 33311.

Career Education: The Newspaper, High Intensity Reading Guide, Grade 3. Career Education Office, School Board of Broward County, 1001 Northwest Fourth St., Ft. Lauderdale, FL 33311.

Megow, Robert; Ripley, Bill; and Arredondo, Patricia. *Newspaper Careers. Occupational Information Package.* Part A, 2nd rev. August 1976. Patricia Arredondo, Office of Career Education, Orange County Public Schools, 410 Woods Ave., Orlando, FL 32805.

Williams, Janet. *Curriculum Guide for Career English.* November 1975. Career Education Office, Instructional Services Offices, 1274 South Florida Ave., Rockledge, FL 32955. Also see Williams, Janet. *What is Career English?,* an informative brochure on the course. ERIC Document Reproduction Service, Arlington, Va. (ED 092 270).

Hawaii

Hawaii Career Development Continuum, Curriculum Guide for Grades K-3. June 1974. (Free to Hawaii teachers.) Career Education Office, Department of Education, 1270 Queen Emma St.—Rm. 902, Honolulu, HA 97813. ERIC Document Reproduction Service, Arlington, Va. (ED 109 319).

Same as above but *for Grades 4-6* (ED 109 320), *for Grades 7-9* (ED 109 321), or *for Grades 10-12* (ED 109 322).

Montana

Montana Career Education Resource Directory: Programs, Planning Guides, Instructional Materials, Community Resources, Funding, AV Resources, Bibliography. July 1978. Career Education Consultant, Office of Public Instruction, Helena, MT 59601.

Oklahoma

Shipp, Jeanetta C. *Career Awareness, K-6: I Can Be Me from A to Z.* 1974. ($4.00) State Department of Vocational and Technical Education, Curriculum and Instructional Materials Center, 1515 W. Sixth Ave., Stillwater, OK 74074.

A Guide for Developmental Vocational Guidance, K-12. Rev. ed. 1973. ($3.00) State Department of Vocational and Technical Education, Guidance and Counseling Section, 1515 W. Sixth Ave., Stillwater, OK 74074.

New Directions in English: Units of Study for Vocational and Employment Bound Students: Tenth, Eleventh or Twelfth Grades. 1974. ($6.00) State Department of Vocational and Technical Education, Curriculum and Instructional Materials Center, 1515 W. Sixth Ave., Stillwater, OK 74074.

Pennsylvania

Getting Started: A Guide to Writing Your Own Curriculum. The Pennsylvania Guide for Instructional Improvement through Career Education. Junior high volume. 1976. ($15.00) Central Susquehanna Intermediate Unit, P.O. Box 213, Lewisburg, PA 17837. ERIC Document Reproduction Service, Arlington, Va. (ED 141 499).

Same as above but senior high volume (ED 141 501).

Rhode Island

Soper, Joan, ed. *A Career Education Idea Book for English Teachers* (Grades 7-12) 1972. Career Education Office, Rhode Island Department of Education, 24 Hayes St., Providence, RI 02908. James Ryan, East Providence School Department, 255 Taunton Ave., East Providence, RI 02914. ERIC Document Reproduction Service, Arlington, Va. (ED 105 168).

Vermont

Cornely, Edward V., ed. *Integration of Career Education Concepts into the High School Curriculum.* State Department of Education, Language Arts Supervisor, Montpelier, VT 05602. ERIC Document Reproduction Service, Arlington, Va. (ED 099 470).

Washington

Communication Skills for Career Education. Junior High/Middle Schools. 1974. Washington State Department of Education. Available only through ERIC Document Reproduction Service, Arlington, Va. (ED 095 389).

Miscellaneous Resources

Real World is a newspaper designed to provide high school students with up-to-date and interesting information about a variety of careers. Published from September through May, the twenty-page paper contains both news articles and in-depth interviews to provide readers with information about all facets of work, including the nature of work, entry-level education and training required, working conditions, salary and job outlook. It excels at featuring new and unusual jobs, as well as non-traditional jobs for women and men. For subscription information about class sets of either fifteen or thirty copies for either one or two semesters, write: King Features Syndicate, Inc., 235 East 45th St., New York, NY 10017.

Two student magazines, *Career World I* (grades 4-7) and *Career World II* (grades 7-12), contain news and feature articles to increase students' awareness of careers. The magazines are published from September through May and subscription information can be obtained from: Curriculum Innovations, Inc., 501 Lake Forest Ave., Highwood, IL 60040.

Career Education Activity Series is available from either ABT Associates, 55 Wheeler St., Cambridge, MA 02138 or ERIC Document Reproduction Service, P.O. Box 190, Arlington, VA 22210.

Lawson, Jane; and Finn, Peter. *Career Education Activities for Subject Area Teachers. Grades 1-6.* May 1975. ED 133 468.

Finn, Peter; and Lawson, Jane. *Career Education Activities for Subject Area Teachers. Grades 6-9.* May 1975. ED 133 469.

Finn, Peter; and Lawson, Jane. *Career Education Activities for Subject Area Teachers. Grades 9-12.* May 1975. ED 133 470.

6 General Career Education Resources

The following bibliographies identify numerous resources concerned with career education in all its aspects. The items listed on subsequent pages have all been found especially valuable for reinforcing a sense of the social importance of career education.

Bailey, Larry J. *Facilitating Career Development: An Annotated Bibliography, Part I.* Springfield: Illinois Board of Vocational Education and Rehabilitation, 1970. Arlington, Va.: ERIC Document Reproduction Service, ED 042 217.

Bailey, Larry J.; Wood, Thomas B.; and Fischmar, Sharon, eds. *Facilitating Career Development: An Annotated Bibliography, Part II.* Carbondale: Southern Illinois University, College of Education, Department of Occupational Education, 1974. Arlington, Va.: ERIC Document Reproduction Service, ED 092 674.

Begle, Elsie P. *Career Education: An Annotated Bibliography for Teachers and Curriculum Developers.* Palo Alto: American Institutes for Research in Behavioral Sciences, January 1973. Arlington, Va.: ERIC Document Reproduction Service, ED 073 297.

Billings, Mary DeWitt; and Rubin, Janet S., eds. *Dealing in Futures: Career Education Materials for Students, Parents and Educators: A Bibliography.* Washington, D.C.: Government Printing Office, 1977. GPO SN 017-080-01721-1 ($1.00). Arlington, Va.: ERIC Document Reproduction Service, ED 141 573.

High, Sidney C.; and Hall, Linda. *Bibliography on Career Education.* Washington, D.C.: U.S. Office of Education, May 1973. Arlington, Va.: ERIC Document Reproduction Service, ED 079 554.

Tiedeman, David V.; Schreiber, Marilyn; and Wessell, Tyrus R., Jr. *Key Resources in Career Education: An Annotated Guide.* DeKalb: Northern Illinois University, ERIC Clearinghouse on

Career Education, for the National Institute of Education, April 1976. Washington, D.C.: Government Printing Office, 1976. GPO SN 017-080-01667-2 ($5.75). Arlington, Va.: ERIC Document Reproduction Service, ED 138 752.

Vocational and Career Education, Subject Bibliography 110. Washington, D.C.: Government Printing Office, 1978. (Free).

Wilder, Dee; Hines, Rella; and Sutton, Susan. *Annotated Bibliography on Career Education: For Administrators.* Knoxville: State Department of Education, and the College of Education, University of Tennessee, 1973. Arlington, Va.: ERIC Document Reproduction Service, ED 084 415.

Wilder, Dee; Hines, Rella; and Sutton Susan. *Annotated Bibliography on Career Education: For Postsecondary Educators.* Knoxville: State Department of Education, and the College of Education, University of Tennessee, 1973. Arlington, Va.: ERIC Document Reproduction Service, ED 084 414.

Wilder, Dee; Hines, Rella; and Sutton, Susan. *Annotated Bibliography on Career Education: For Secondary Educators.* Knoxville: State Department of Education, and the College of Education, University of Tennessee, 1973. Arlington, Va.: ERIC Document Reproduction Service, ED 084 413.

York, Edwin G. *1900 Doctoral Dissertations on Career Education.* Edison, N.J.: State Department of Education, June 1975. Arlington, Va.: ERIC Document Reproduction Service, ED 212 933.

Books and Booklets

Books

Bailey, Larry J.; and Stadt, Ronald W. *Career Education: New Approaches to Human Development.* Bloomington, Ill.: McKnight, 1974.

Calhoun, Calfrey C.; and Finch, Alton V. *Vocational and Career Education: Concepts and Operations.* Belmont, Calif.: Wadsworth, 1976.

Evans, Rupert N.; Hoyt, Kenneth B.; and Mangum, Garth L. *Career Education in the Middle/Junior High School.* Salt Lake City: Olympus, 1973.

Fuller, Jack; and Whealon, Terry, eds. *Career Education: A Lifelong Process.* Chicago: Nelson-Hall, 1979.

Goldhammer, Keith; and Taylor, Robert E., eds. *Career Education: Perspective and Promise*. Columbus, Ohio: Charles E. Merrill, 1972.

Herr, Edwin L. *Review and Synthesis of the Foundations for Career Education*. Columbus: Center for Vocational and Technical Education, Ohio State University, 1972. Arlington, Va.: ERIC Document Reproduction Service, ED 059 402.

Hoyt, Kenneth B. *Career Education: Contributions to an Evolving Concept*. Salt Lake City: Olympus, 1975.

Hoyt, Kenneth B.; Evans, Rupert N.; Mackin, Edward F.; and Mangum, Garth L. *Career Education: What It Is and How to Do It*. 2nd ed. Salt Lake City: Olympus, 1974.

Hoyt, Kenneth B.; and Hebeler, Jean R. *Career Education for Gifted and Talented Students*. Salt Lake City: Olympus, 1974.

Hoyt, Kenneth B.; and Mangum, Garth L. *Career Education in the High School*. Salt Lake City: Olympus, 1977.

Hoyt, Kenneth B.; Pinson, Nancy M.; Laramore, Daryl; and Mangum, Garth L. *Career Education and the Elementary School Teacher*. Salt Lake City: Olympus, 1973.

McClure, Larry; and Buan, Carolyn, eds. *Essays in Career Education*. Portland, Ore.: Northwest Regional Development Laboratories, 1973.

Magisos, Joel H., ed. *Career Education: Third Yearbook of the American Vocational Association*. Washington, D.C.: American Vocational Association, 1973.

Mangum, Garth L.; Becker, James W.; Coombs, Garn; and Marshall, Pat, eds. *Career Education in the Academic Classroom*. Salt Lake City: Olympus, 1975.

Marland, Sidney P. *Career Education: A Proposal for Reform*. New York: McGraw-Hill, 1974.

Mitchell, Joyce Slayton. *The Classroom Teacher's Workbook for Career Education*. New York: Avon Books, 1979.

Pautler, Albert J.; Roeder, John A.; Lahren, James A.; and Sugarman, Michael B., eds. *Career Education: Purpose, Function, Goals*. New York: Manuscript Information Corporation, 1973.

Pucinski, Roman; and Pearlman Hirsch, Sharlene, eds. *The Courage to Change: New Directions for Career Education*. Englewood Cliffs, N.J.: Prentice-Hall, 1971.

Ryan, Charles W. *Career Education: A Handbook of Funding Resources.* 5th ed. Boston: Houghton Mifflin, 1979.

Wigglesworth, David C., ed. *Career Education: A Reader.* San Francisco: Canfield Press, 1975.

Booklets

Bell, Terrel H.; and Hoyt, Kenneth B. *Career Education: The USOE Perspective.* Columbus Center for Vocational and Technical Education, Ohio State University, 1974. Arlington, Va.: ERIC Document Reproduction Service, ED 110 596.

Career Education: A Handbook for Implementation. Washington, D.C.: Government Printing Office, 1974. GPO SN 017-080-00926-1 ($1.10).

Hoyt, Kenneth B. *An Introduction to Career Education: A Policy Paper of the United States Office of Education.* Washington, D.C.: Government Printing Office, 1975. GPO SN 017-080-01388-6 ($1.05). Arlington, Va.: ERIC Document Reproduction Service, ED 130 076.

Government Publications

Career Education Monograph Series

Since 1975 the U.S. Office of Education has produced important papers on various aspects of career education in a continuing monograph series. The monographs contain original, unpublished essays as well as reprints of essays and speeches. The monographs are written by Kenneth B. Hoyt, Director, Office of Career Education (OCE), or by classroom teachers, counselors, administrators, and researchers.

The list of titles given below is current as of 1978. Titles and prices of all monographs can be obtained from both OCE and the ERIC Document Reproduction Service. Individual copies can be ordered from two sources: (1) Superintendent of Documents, U.S. Government Printing Office, Washington, DC 20402; and (2) ERIC Document Reproduction Service, P.O. Box 190, Arlington, VA 22210. Public inquiries regarding document ordering can be made by calling (202) 783-3238. Earlier titles that are out of print are available only through ERIC.

The Career Education Monographs are listed, with prices, in ERIC's monthly catalog *Resources in Education* under "Office of

Career Education" as the institutional author and "Career Education" as the subject descriptor. Abstracts of monographs can be found in the catalog, and complete monographs can be read in microfiche form wherever the ERIC collection is housed. One has only to cite the ERIC document (ED) number to locate the document in the microfiche card catalog. The monographs are also listed in monthly catalogs of the Government Printing Office, which are available at government depository libraries, often located in university libraries and public libraries in larger cities.

Chenault, Joann. *Career Education and Human Services.* Washington, D.C.: Government Printing Office, 1977. GPO SN 017-080-01741-5 ($1.30). Arlington, Va.: ERIC Document Reproduction Service, ED 109 507.

Chanault, Joann; and Mermis, W. L. *The Professional Education of Human Services Personnel.* Washington, D.C.: Government Printing Office, 1976. Arlington, Va.: ERIC Document Reproduction Service, ED 130 108.

Datta, Lois-ellin, et al. *Career Education: What Proof Do We Have That It Works?* Washington, D.C.: Government Printing Office, 1977. GPO SN 017-080-01785-7 ($2.10). Arlington, Va.: ERIC Document Reproduction Service, ED 151 516.

Enderlein, Thomas E. *A Review of Career Education Evaluation Studies.* Washington, D.C.: Government Printing Office, 1975. GPO SN 017-080-01686-9 ($1.40). Arlington, Va.: ERIC Document Reproduction Service, ED 141 584.

Evans, Rupert N. *Career Education and Vocational Education: Similarities and Contrasts.* Washington, D.C.: Government Printing Office, 1975. GPO SN 017-080-01742-3 ($1.10). Arlington, Va.: ERIC Document Reproduction Service, ED 127 472.

Herr, Edwin L. *The British Experience in Educational Change, Careers Education, School Counselor Role and Counselor Training: Implications for American Education.* Washington, D.C.: Government Printing Office, 1977. GPO SN 017-080-01702-4 ($1.70). Arlington, Va.: ERIC Document Reproduction Service, ED 142 846.

Herr, Edwin L.; and Cramer, Stanley H. *Conditions in Education Calling for Reform: An Analysis.* Washington, D.C.: Government Printing Office, 1975. GPO SN 017-080-01743-1 ($1.90). Arlington, Va.: ERIC Document Reproduction Service, ED 109 508.

Hoyt, Kenneth B. *Applications of the Concept of Career Educa-tion to Higher Education: An Idealistic Model.* Washington, D.C.: Government Printing Office, 1976. GPO SN 017-080-01617-6 ($0.45). Arlington, Va.: ERIC Document Reproduction Service, ED 130 085.

Hoyt, Kenneth B. *Career Education and the Business-Labor-Industry Community.* Washington, D.C.: Government Print-ing Office, 1976. GPO SN 017-080-01613-3 ($0.45). Arlington, Va.: ERIC Document Reproduction Service, ED 146 461.

Hoyt, Kenneth B. *Career Education: Implications for Counselors.* Washington, D.C.: Government Printing Office, 1977. GPO SN 017-080-01619-2 ($0.55). Arlington, Va.: ERIC Document Re-production Service, ED 134 821.

Hoyt, Kenneth B. *Career Education and Organized Labor.* Washington, D.C.: Government Printing Office, 1979. GPO SN 017-080-01945-1. Arlington, Va.: ERIC Document Reproduction Service, ED 164 983.

Hoyt, Kenneth B. *Career Education for Special Populations.* Washington, D.C.: Government Printing Office, 1976. GPO SN 017-080-01612-5 ($0.45). Arlington, Va.: ERIC Document Re-production Service, ED 132 428.

Hoyt, Kenneth B. *Chambers of Commerce and Career Education.* Washington, D.C.: Government Printing Office, 1978. GPO SN 017-080-01893-4 ($1.40). Arlington, Va.: ERIC Document Re-production Service, ED 162 568.

Hoyt, Kenneth B. *Community Resources for Career Education.* Washington, D.C.: Government Printing Office, 1976. GPO SN 017-080-01615-0 ($0.55). Arlington, Va.: ERIC Document Re-production Service, ED 130 118.

Hoyt, Kenneth B. *Conception of Collaboration in Career Educa-tion.* Washington, D.C.: Government Printing Office, 1978. GPO SN 017-080-0189-8 ($2.20). Arlington, Va.: ERIC Docu-ment Reproduction Service, ED 164 861.

Hoyt, Kenneth B. *Considerations of Career Education in Post-secondary Education.* Washington, D.C.: Government Printing Office, 1978. GPO SN 017-080-01892-6 ($1.90).

Hoyt, Kenneth B. *Exploring Division, Boy Scouts of America, Girl Scouts of the USA, and Career Education.* Washington, D.C.: Government Printing Office, 1978. GPO SN 017-080-01902-7 ($1.50). Arlington, Va.: ERIC Document Reproduction Service, ED 167 806.

Hoyt, Kenneth B. *4-H and Career Education.* Washington, D.C.: Government Printing Office, 1978. GPO SN 017-080-01894-2 ($1.50). Arlington, Va.: ERIC Document Reproduction Service, ED 162 159.

Hoyt, Kenneth B. *Future Farmers of America and Career Education.* Washington, D.C.: Government Printing Office, 1978. GPO SN 017-080-01922-1 ($1.50). Arlington, Va.: ERIC Document Reproduction Service, ED 167 807.

Hoyt, Kenneth B. *Junior Achievement, Inc., and Career Education.* Washington, D.C.: Government Printing Office, 1978. GPO SN 017-080-01890-9 ($1.50). Arlington, Va.: ERIC Document Reproduction Service, ED 164 835.

Hoyt, Kenneth B. *K-12 Classroom Teachers and Career Education: The Beautiful People.* Washington, D.C.: Government Printing Office, 1976. GPO SN 017-080-01537-4 ($0.90). Arlington, Va.: ERIC Document Reproduction Service, ED 130 034.

Hoyt, Kenneth B. *National Alliance of Business and Career Education.* Washington, D.C.: Government Printing Office, June 1978. GPO SN 017-080-01888-8 ($1.40). Arlington, Va.: ERIC Document Reproduction Service, ED 162 160.

Hoyt, Kenneth B. *The National Federation of Business and Professional Women's Clubs and Career Education.* Washington, D.C.: Government Printing Office, 1978. GPO SN 017-080-01920-5 ($1.40). Arlington, Va.: ERIC Document Reproduction Service, ED 167 809.

Hoyt, Kenneth B. *Perspectives on the Problem of Evaluation in Career Education.* Washington, D.C.: Government Printing Office, 1976. GPO SN 017-080-01745-8 ($1.60). Arlington, Va.: ERIC Document Reproduction Service, ED 127 471.

Hoyt, Kenneth B. *A Primer for Career Education.* Washington, D.C.: Government Printing Office, 1977. GPO SN 017-080-01752-1 ($1.50). Arlington, Va.: ERIC Document Reproduction Service, ED 145 252.

Hoyt, Kenneth B. *Refining the Career Education Concept.* Washington, D.C.: Government Printing Office, 1976. GPO SN 017-080-01610-9 ($1.75). Arlington, Va.: ERIC Document Reproduction Service, ED 132 427.

Hoyt, Kenneth B. *Refining the Career Education Concept, Part II.* Washington, D.C.: Government Printing Office, 1977. GPO SN 017-080-01739-3 ($1.50). Arlington, Va.: ERIC Document Reproduction Service, ED 146 362.

Hoyt, Kenneth B. *Refining the Career Education Concept, Part III.* Washington, D.C.: Government Printing Office, 1978. GPO SN 017-080-01887-0 ($2.20). Arlington, Va.: ERIC Document Reproduction Service, ED 164 860.

Hoyt, Kenneth B. *Refining the Concept of Collaboration in Career Education.* Washington, D.C.: Government Printing Office, 1978. GPO SN 017-080-01986-8 ($1.90). Arlington, Va.: ERIC Document Reproduction Service, ED 167 808.

Hoyt, Kenneth B. *Relationships between Career Education and Vocational Education.* Washington, D.C.: Government Printing Office, 1976. GPO SN 017-080-01614-1 ($0.75). Arlington, Va.: ERIC Document Reproduction Service, ED 132 367.

Hoyt, Kenneth B. *Rotary International and Career Education.* Washington, D.C.: Government Printing Office, 1978. GPO SN 017-080-01921-3 ($1.50). Arlington, Va.: ERIC Document Reproduction Service, ED 171 930.

Hoyt, Kenneth B. *The School Counselor and Career Education.* Washington, D.C.: Government Printing Office, 1976. GPO SN 017-080-01528-5 ($0.55). Arlington, Va.: ERIC Document Reproduction Service, ED 134 905.

Hoyt, Kenneth B. *Teachers and Career Education.* Washington, D.C.: Government Printing Office, 1976. GPO SN 017-080-01618-4 ($0.70). Arlington, Va.: ERIC Document Reproduction Service, ED 131 281.

Hoyt, Kenneth B. *Women's American ORT and Career Education.* Washington, D.C.: Government Printing Office, 1979. GPO SN 017-080-01904-3 ($1.50). Arlington, Va.: ERIC Document Reproduction Service, ED 164 859.

Hoyt, Kenneth B. *YEPDA and Career Education.* Washington, D.C.: Government Printing Office, 1978. GPO SN 017-080-01889-6 ($2.10). Arlington, Va.: ERIC Document Reproduction Service, ED 160 793.

Jackson, Roberta H. *Career Education and the Minorities.* Washington, D.C.: Government Printing Office, 1977. GPO SN 017-080-01733-4 ($2.75). Arlington, Va.: ERIC Document Reproduction Service, ED 149 126.

Moore, Charles G. *Baby Boom Equals Career Bust.* Washington, D.C.: Government Printing Office, 1977. GPO SN 017-080-01758-0 ($1.10). Arlington, Va.: ERIC Document Reproduction Service, ED 146 411.

Olson, Paul A. *The Liberal Arts and Career Education: A Look at the Past and the Future.* Washington, D.C.: Government Printing Office, 1975. GPO SN 017-080-01744-0 ($1.30). Arlington, Va.: ERIC Document Reproduction Service, ED 113 487.

O'Toole, James. *The Reserve Army of the Underemployed.* Washington, D.C.: Government Printing Office, 1975. GPO SN 017-080-01746-6 ($1.30). Arlington, Va.: ERIC Document Reproduction Service, ED 109 509.

Preli, Barbara. *Career Education and the Teaching/Learning Process.* Washington, D.C.: Government Printing Office, 1978. GPO SN 017-080-01849-7 ($1.50). Arlington, Va.: ERIC Document Reproduction Service, ED 159 355.

Super, Donald E. *Career Education and the Meanings of Work.* Washington, D.C.: Government Printing Office, 1976. GPO SN 017-080-01554-4 ($0.70). Arlington, Va.: ERIC Document Reproduction Service, ED 128 593.

Department of Labor Career Materials

The U.S. Department of Labor produces many publications and film resources that relate to career education. Several of these materials—such as posters, brochures, books, and films—are typically found in school guidance and counseling offices, but they make excellent supplementary resources for classroom instruction. They provide students with a wealth of information on occupations. Following are some of the resources that might be helpful for use with students. All of these materials are available as indicated, either from the Superintendent of Documents, U.S. Government Printing Office, Washington, DC 20402 or from any of the eight regional offices of the Bureau of Labor Statistics, at the addresses shown below. Because prices are not always listed, and those quoted are subject to change. it is advisable to write in advance to determine prices.

Bureau of Labor Statistics Regional Offices:

1603 Federal Office Bldg., Boston, MA 02203

1515 Broadway, New York, NY 10036

P.O. Box 13309, Philadelphia, PA 19101

1371 Peachtree St. NE, Atlanta, GA 30309

230 South Dearborn St., Chicago, IL 60604

555 Griffin Sq. Bldg., Dallas, TX 75202

911 Walnut St., Kansas City, MO 64106

450 Golden Gate Ave., Box 36017, San Francisco, CA 94102

Occupational Outlook Handbook. 1980–1981 ed., paper (GPO SN 029-001-02059-7) $8.00; hardcover (GPO SN 029-001-01067) $11.00. Superintendent of Documents.

This encyclopedia of careers provides over eight hundred pages of information about the occupational outlook, training, educational requirements, and working conditions of several hundred occupations and over thirty-five industries. Published every two years, the handbook is up to date, accurate, easy and interesting to read, and serves as a quick reference for students who are conducting research on careers.

Occupational Outlook Quarterly. One year $6.00. Superintendent of Documents.

This periodical is issued to keep young people, guidance counselors, and others abreast of current occupational and employment developments occurring between editions of the *Occupational Outlook Handbook.*

Looking Ahead to a Career. 1978–1979 ed. $12.50. Regional offices, Bureau of Labor Statistics

A 27 minute 35 mm color filmstrip and accompanying tape cassette narrative that provides viewers with charts, cartoons, and photographs to explain the career cluster system, industrial and occupational trends, and the employment outlook for college graduates.

Exploring Careers. Bulletin 2001. 1979. Available in one volume, 550 pp., paper (GPO SN 029-001-02224-7) $10.00; or in fifteen booklets (GPO SN 029-001-0222-5) $12.00. Superintendent of Documents or regional offices, Bureau of Labor Statistics.

A new career guidance publication for junior high or middle school students which can be used in classrooms, career resource centers, and community youth programs. The 600-page book introduces students to various occupations within fourteen career clusters and emphasizes what people do on the job and how they feel about their work. Each chapter contains a narrative description of the cluster and photographs of men and women in their work settings. Questions, activities, and career games are also suggested.

Leaflets and Posters

Career-oriented leaflets and posters for classroom use are available from the regional offices of the Bureau of Labor Statistics.

National Advisory Council for Career Education Publications

Arterbury, Elvis H. *The Efficacy of Career Education, Career Awareness.* Washington, D.C.: Government Printing Office, 1975. Arlington, Va.: ERIC Document Reproduction Service, ED 121 953.

Aubrey, Roger F. *Career Development Needs of Thirteen-Year-Olds.* Washington, D.C.: Government Printing Office, 1977. GPO SN 017-080-01790-3. Arlington, Va.: ERIC Document Reproduction Service, ED 147 498.

Berke, Joel S.; and Hartle, Terry W. *Analysis and Synthesis of Existing Career Education Legislation.* Washington, D.C.: Government Printing Office. Arlington, Va.: ERIC Document Reproduction Service, ED 122 009.

Berke, Joel S.; and Hartle, Terry W. *Key Concepts in Career Education: Legislative and Policy Issues.* Washington, D.C.: Government Printing Office, 1975. Arlington, Va.: ERIC Document Reproduction Service, ED 122 010.

Bryant, Rita. *The Efficacy of Career Education, Academic Achievement.* Washington, D.C.: Government Printing Office, 1975. Arlington, Va.: ERIC Document Reproduction Service, ED 122 003.

Goldstein, Michael B. *The Current State of Career Education at the Postsecondary Level.* Washington, D.C.: Government Printing Office, 1977. GPO SN 017-080-01734-2 ($2.75). Arlington, Va.: ERIC Document Reproduction Service, ED 141 610.

Hansen, Lorraine Sundal. *An Examination of the Definitions and Concepts of Career Education.* Washington, D.C.: Government Printing Office, 1977. GPO SN 017-080-01738-5 ($2.50). Arlington, Va.: ERIC Document Reproduction Service, ED 141 609.

Hartle, Terry W. *The Implementation and Administration of a Federal Career Education Program.* Washington, D.C.: Government Printing Office, 1975. Arlington, Va.: ERIC Document Reproduction Service, ED 122 008.

Hensley, Gene; and Schulman, Mark. *Two Studies on the Role of Business and Industry and Labor Participation in Career Education.* Washington, D.C.: Government Printing Office,

1977. GPO SN 017-080-01737-7 ($2.75). Arlington, Va.: ERIC Document Reproduction Service, ED 141 608.

Herr, Edwin L. *The Emerging History of Career Education: A Summary View.* Washington, D.C.: Government Printing Office, 1976. Arlington, Va.: ERIC Document Reproduction Service, ED 122 011.

Jesser, David L. *An Analysis of State Laws on Career Education and Pending State Legislation.* Washington, D.C.: Government Printing Office, 1975. Arlington, Va.: ERIC Document Reproduction Service, ED 122 006.

Katz, Martin R.; Miller-Tiedeman, Anna; Osipow, Samuel H.; and Tiedeman, David V. *The Cross-sectional Story of Early Career Development as Revealed by the National Assessment of Educational Progress.* Washington, D.C.: Government Printing Office, 1977. GPO SN 017-080-01782-2. Arlington, Va.: ERIC Document Reproduction Service, ED 147 490.

Marland, Sidney P. *Career Education Update.* Washington, D.C.: Government Printing Office, 1976. Arlington, Va.: ERIC Document Reproduction Service, ED 133 513.

Marland, Sidney P. *National Advisory Council for Career Education: Interim Report with Recommendations for Legislation, 1975.* Washington, D.C.: Government Printing Office, 1975. GPO SN 017-080-01498-0 ($0.85). Arlington, Va.: ERIC Document Reproduction Service, ED 112 268.

Masucci, Michael J. *The Efficacy of Career Education, Career Decision-making.* Washington, D.C.: Government Printing Office, 1975. Arlington, Va.: ERIC Document Reproduction Service, ED 122 004.

Miller, Juliet V. *Career Development Needs of Nine-Year-Olds: How to Improve Career Development Programs.* Washington, D.C.: Government Printing Office, 1977. GPO SN 017-080-01788-1. Arlington, Va.: ERIC Document Reproduction Service, ED 147 497.

Mitchell, Anita M. *Career Development Needs of Seventeen-Year Olds: How to Improve Career Development Programs.* Washington, D.C.: Government Printing Office, 1977. GPO SN 017-080-01810-1 ($3.25). Arlington, Va.: ERIC Document Reproduction Service, ED 147 555.

National Advisory Council for Career Education. *The Efficacy of Career Education.* (A summary of publications by E. H. Arterbury, R. Bryant, M. J. Masucci, and C. R. Schager, cited separately in this series.) Washington, D.C.: Government Printing Office, 1976. Arlington, Va.: ERIC Document Reproduction Service, ED 130 092.

National Advisory Council for Career Education. *Interim Report of the National Advisory Council for Career Education.* Washington, D.C.: Government Printing Office, 1976. GPO SN 017-080-01701-6. Arlington, Va.: ERIC Document Reproduction Service, ED 141 626.

National Advisory Council for Career Education. *Next Steps in Career Education.* (A summary of papers by John Porter, Sidney P. Marland, Harold Hodgkinson, Larry Bailey, Kenneth B. Hoyt, and Charles Heatherly.) Washington, D.C.: Government Printing Office, 1976. GPO SN 017-080-01703-2 ($1.60). Arlington, Va.: ERIC Document Reproduction Service, ED 141 574.

Rosen, David Paul; Olson, Layton; and Cox, Karen. *Masters of Reality: Certificate or Performance? Towards Policy and Practice for Postsecondary Education and Work Programs Based on Outcomes for Students.* Washington, D.C.: Government Printing Office, 1977. Arlington, Va.: ERIC Document Reproduction Service, ED 138 810.

Schager, Cherylynn Risch. *The Efficacy of Career Education, Other Ways of Assessing Effectiveness.* Washington, D.C.: Government Printing Office. Arlington, Va.: ERIC Document Reproduction Service, ED 122 005.

Sexton, Robert F. *Experiential Education and Community Involvement Practices at the Postsecondary Level: Implications for Career Education.* Washington, D.C.: Government Printing Office, 1977. GPO SN 017-080-01735-1 ($2.10). Arlington, Va.: ERIC Document Reproduction Service, ED 138 771.

Smith, Keith E. *A Summary of Commissioned Papers Prepared for the National Advisory Council for Career Education.* Washington, D.C.: Government Printing Office, 1976. Arlington, Va.: ERIC Document Reproduction Service, ED 128 661.

Valley, John R. *Career Education of Adults.* Washington, D.C.: Government Printing Office, 1977. GPO SN 017-080-01736-9 ($2.20). Arlington, Va.: ERIC Document Reproduction Service, ED 141 611.

Wasdyke, Raymond G. *Career Education and the Future.* Washington, D.C.: Government Printing Office, 1975. Arlington, Va.: ERIC Document Reproduction Service, ED 122 007.

Westbrook, Bert W. *Career Development Needs of Adults: How to Improve Career Development Programs.* Washington, D.C.: Government Printing Office, 1977. GPO SN 017-080-01787-3 .($2.10). Arlington, Va.: ERIC Document Reproduction Service, ED 147 499.

Worthington, Robert M. *Review and Synthesis of Research Concerning Career Education in Doctoral Dissertations of Fellows Supported by the Education Professions Development Act, Section 552, 1972–1975.* Princeton: Career Development Associates, Inc., for the National Advisory Council for Career Education, 1975. Arlington, Va.: ERIC Document Reproduction Service, ED 117 401.

National Institute of Education Publications

The publications listed below are issued by the National Institute of Education. The first is an independent publication; those following are from the series "Papers in Education and Work." Single copies of the series are available free from the Institute or, for a fee, from ERIC Document Reproduction Service. Cite the appropriate ED numbers when ordering from ERIC. Addresses are as follows:

National Institute of Education, Publications Office, Brown Building, 19th and M Sts., NW, Washington, DC 20208

ERIC Document Reproduction Service, P.O. Box 190, Arlington, VA 22210

Bridgeford, Nancy; Clark, Marilyn; and McClure, Larry. *Directions in Career Education: Questions People Ask about Education and Work.* 1977. ED 154 160.

Papers in Education and Work

Barton, Paul E.; Bobrow, Sue B.; and Walsh, John J. *Industry/Education Councils.* No. 9, 1977. ED 155 487.

Fox, Lynn H.; Fennema, Elizabeth; and Sherman, Julia. *Women and Mathematics: Research Perspectives for Change.* No. 8, November 1977. ED 160 403.

Gibboney Associates, Richard A. *The Career Intern Program: Final Report. Volume I: An Experiment in Career Education That Worked.* No. 7, May 1977. ED 117 351.

Gibboney Associates, Richard A. *The Career Intern Program: Final Report. Volume II. Technical Appendices.* No. 7, May 1977. ED 118 868.

Gill, William B.; and Luke, Ann W. *Facilities Handbook for Career Education.* No. 2, October 1976. ED 131 550.

Kurland, Norman D. *Entitlement Papers.* No. 4, March 1977. ED 138 164.

Leifer, Aimee Dorr; and Lesser, Gerald S. *The Development of Career Awareness in Young Children.* No. 1, October 1976. ED 121 299.

Levine, Herbert A. *Paid Educational Leave.* No. 6, March 1977. ED 140 022.

Quinn, Robert P.; and Baldi de Mandilovitch, Martha S. *Education and Job Satisfaction: A Questionable Payoff.* No. 5, March 1977. ED 117 327.

Timpano, Doris M.; and Knight, Louise W. *Sex Discrimination in the Selection of School District Administrators: What Can Be Done?* No. 3, December 1976. ED 133 917.

Author

Jan E. Kilby is Director, Educational Placement Office, University of Illinois at Urbana-Champaign. Prior to her directorship of the NCTE Project on Career Education, she received her Ph.D. in Curriculum and Instruction from the University of Texas at Austin. Her dissertation is titled, "A Career Education Program for English and English Education Majors in Colleges and Universities." She is a member of the NCTE Conference on English Education and the Association for Supervision and Curriculum Development.